D0725302

Kubrick Red: A Memoir

ABOUT THE AUTHOR

Simon Roy teaches literature at Collège Lionel-Groulx,
in Sainte-Thérèse, Quebec.

Kubrick Red: A Memoir is his first book.

SiMON ROY

KUBRiCK

RED

Translated by Jacob Homel

NOT FOR RESALE
REVIEW PURPOSES ONLY

ANVIL PRESS • VANCOUVER • 2016

Copyright © 2014 by Simon Roy
Translation Copyright © 2016 by Jacob Homel

Originally published in French under the title *Ma vie rouge Kubrick*, Les Éditions du
Boréal, 2015.

All rights reserved. No part of this book may be reproduced by any means without
the prior written permission of the publisher, with the exception of brief passages
in reviews. Any request for photocopying or other reprographic copying of any part
of this book must be directed in writing to access: The Canadian Copyright Licens-
ing Agency, One Yonge Street, Suite 800, Toronto, Ontario, Canada, M5E 1E5.

Anvil Press Publishers Inc.
P.O. Box 3008, Main Post Office
Vancouver, B.C. V6B 3X5 CANADA
www.anvilpress.com

Library and Archives Canada Cataloguing in Publication

Roy, Simon, 1968-
[Ma vie rouge Kubrick. English]
    Kubrick red : a memoir / Simon Roy ; Jacob Homel, translator.

Translation of: Ma vie rouge Kubrick.
ISBN 978-1-77214-072-9 (paperback)

    1. Roy, Simon, 1968- --Family. 2. Kubrick, Stanley--Criticism
and interpretation. 3. Shining (Motion picture). 4. Mothers--Suicidal
behavior. I. Homel, Jacob, 1987-, translator II. Title. III. Title: Ma
vie rouge Kubrick. English.

PS8635.O911543M3813 2016   C844'.6   C2016-906985-0

Printed and bound in Canada
Cover design by Rayola Graphic
Interior by HeimatHouse
Represented in Canada by Publishers Group Canada
Distributed by Raincoast Books

We acknowledge the financial support of the Government of Canada, through the
National Translation Program for Book Publishing for our translation activities.

The publisher gratefully acknowledges the financial assistance of the Canada
Council for the Arts, the Canada Book Fund, and the Province of British Columbia
through the B.C. Arts Council and the Book Publishing Tax Credit.

To my mother Danielle.
Thank you for everything.
Thank you despite everything.

it rushes over me
on an exit ramp
back from work
at the wheel of the car
a song she used to sing
in a grocery store aisle
I think of my mother
and I'm breathless
I so wish I could
still tell her and still hear her

—Bruno Lemieux
Dans le ventre la nuit, 2013

How'd you like some ice cream, Doc?

"It's a horror story even for people who don't like horror stories—maybe especially for them." (From Bruce McCabe's review of *The Shining* in the *Boston Globe* in 1980. Published on my birthday: June 14.)

The word *shining* is sometimes used to indicate a paranormal phenomenon, usually related to telepathy. Like a strange state of *luminescence*. It's said that past events sometimes leave furrows in their wake and individuals with a very particular gift, those with the *shining*, can perceive them.

*   *   *

I was ten or twelve, no more than that, when I first saw *The Shining*. I saw the French version on television. Called *L'enfant lumière* in French, Child of Light. At that age, I had no idea who Jack Nicholson or Stanley Kubrick were. However, a few years earlier, I'd seen Shelley Duvall in an adaptation of *Popeye* at the Joliette movie theatre with my mother. Robin Williams in the titular role; Duvall played Olive Oyl.

It was a warm, humid summer night. From inside the house, I could hear crickets chirping through the wide open windows. It was late, a little after the ten o'clock news. My mother had left me alone; she was off visiting friends of hers, a couple, who lived on the other side of the street from our small bungalow. They'd be playing cards together, like every other Saturday night, games that sometimes dragged on through the middle of the night. With a bowl of chips between my legs, I was flipping through the channels, idle as only a ten- or twelve-year-old can be, alone, at such a late hour.

Completely by chance, as I flipped through the channels, I ended up on a scene in the movie. A small boy with the same square haircut as I had at the time, throwing darts at a target. I have no clear memory of the beginning of the film. Not even the mysterious Grady sisters. And yet, I can clearly remember having hurried to my mother's card game on the other side of the street right after having watched the scene—which wasn't even that scary—where Dick Hallorann, as he gives a tour of the storeroom to Mrs. Torrance and the boy, turns to the child and asks him in a distorted, slow-motion voice "How'd you like some ice cream, Doc?" all the while continuing his enumeration of the stocked goods to Wendy Torrance.

The doubling of chef Hallorann's voice created in me such powerful unease that I can still feel it, intact, thirty years later. We don't choose our memories, and that one in particular imprinted itself on my mind in a process akin to the formation of fossils. It didn't matter that I knew they were only images on the television set, a noxious feeling grew in me anyway, as if the black man had spoken those words to me alone. As if he named me with his dark eyes instead of the boy named Danny, the boy who, for that matter, had remained a little ways off, in the door frame to the refrigerated room. For some unknown reason, even though I couldn't possibly be that naïve at that age, I felt like Hallorann had for a moment drawn back from his role as the guide to the Overlook Hotel to establish a direct relationship with me and reveal something hidden. A revelation that went far beyond a cordial invitation to savour a bowl of chocolate ice cream. I stared at Dick Hallorann's lips, and it was as if they detached themselves from his strong black face to spit words at me, shaking me to the core. Was that what they called the *shining*?

A chink in the armour of my comfortable childhood. *For ever, and ever, and ever.* Through *The Shining*, horror entered my life. A life which had, until then, been safeguarded by a mother always ready to overprotect me from the threats of the outside world. Who could have blamed her?

And so my first experience with the movie that created such an extraordinary fascination in me was cut short. No one knows that, still today, I sometimes hear my own voice ringing in my head when I open the freezer door: *"How'd you like some ice cream, Doc?"*

The Caretaker of the Overlook Hotel

Cast: Jack Nicholson (Jack Torrance)
Shelley Duvall (Wendy Torrance)
Danny Lloyd (Danny Torrance)

Jack Torrance and his family (his wife, Wendy, and their seven-year-old son, Danny) have recently moved to Colorado. A former teacher at Stovington Prep in Vermont, Jack is looking for a job which will offer him the requisite time to work on his current project: he wants to write a novel. The opportunity at the Overlook Hotel seems like a perfect fit. At first, the whole thing seems rather simple: essentially taking care of the hotel and doing maintenance during the winter season, during which the road to the hotel is completely snowed in. Stuart Ullman, the hotel's manager, takes pains during the job interview to tell Jack that the establishment still bears the burden of a tragedy which occurred ten years earlier. A former caretaker, a man named Grady, murdered his wife and two daughters with an axe before blowing his brains out. For some, solitude and isolation can be difficult to deal with. Even if he's a little put off by the story, Jack takes the job.

Meanwhile, Danny, his son, has catastrophic premonitions about the hotel. The boy falls prey to frightening visions that send him into a trancelike state. He sees, among other things, waves of blood bursting forth from an elevator shaft, two girls holding each other by the hand, motionless, twins it seems, dressed in matching azure dresses. But the die is cast, Jack and his family will spend the winter in the luxurious hotel perched atop a mountain in Colorado.

As soon as the Torrances arrive at the Overlook, the hotel's management gives them the grand tour. Wendy is impressed by its labyrinthine corridors, a characteristic echoed by an immense maze formed by tall cedar hedges on the hotel's grounds. The three solitary pensioners seem a bit lost in the vast hotel akin to a *ghost ship*.

After a first few idyllic weeks spent relaxing, unease begins building in Jack. His mind begins to flicker. At first, only light symptoms can be detected, indications that he might not be as stable as we first thought. If we sometimes witness him writing in the Overlook's main drawing room, sitting at his typewriter, he's often seen idling, throwing a tennis ball against the walls, staring blankly at other walls, or studying a model of the hotel grounds' cedar maze in the Colorado Lounge.

Locked in the hermetic cell of the novel he's writing, Jack Torrance becomes increasingly distant. His only interactions with the other members of his family become increasingly tense, charged with worrying undertones.

Parallel to this, the child, left to his own devices, explores the Overlook's deserted hallways, moving about on a Big Wheel tricycle, or playing with his miniature cars. However, guided by a vision, Danny develops an unhealthy curiosity about one room in particular at the Overlook. Room 237. An echo of the forbidden room in the fairy tale *Bluebeard*. The child can't help himself: he needs to explore the room. He will end up entering it, a bit like the too-curious princesses in Charles Perrault's story who secretly defied the injunctions of their murderous tyrant; *curiosity killed the cat.*

While the plot up to this point has moved to the rhythm of a psychological thriller, exploiting the unease of the characters and the viewer, a rhythm closer to that of a slasher movie now kicks into gear. The father begins to believe that he must kill his child, encouraged by the spirits and demons of the Overlook. There begins a clearly homicidal hunt. Armed with an axe, the father stalks the haunted corridors of the hotel, mouth frothing and madness in his eyes, looking for his wife and his son. His intentions seem clear: for them to suffer the same fate as the Grady sisters, executed by their father's hand, the former caretaker, some ten years earlier.

The child finds refuge in the gigantic cedar maze near the hotel, hunted by his mad father who is determined to fulfill his sacrificial mission. A snowstorm inspires Danny to try a ruse: he hides behind a cedar row and wipes away his footsteps in the snow with his hand, confounding Jack, who, now raving mad, loses himself both in the maze and in his mind, howling the name of his son to the stars above, like a wolf in the night. Danny uses this moment to flee the maze, retracing his footsteps. He reunites with his mother, still safe and sound. She finds a small tracked vehicle, and they make their way to the closest city, Sidewinder.

Jack dies after a night of wandering among the snow-filled paths of his green maze.

A Very Critical Reception

The *Shining* was poorly received upon its release. It was nominated for worst director (Stanley Kubrick) and worst actress (Shelley Duvall) at the very first celebration of the *Razzies* (The Golden Raspberry Awards), a sort of anti-Oscars which aims to highlight the worst of the worst in the world of movies.

The website *Metacritic* gives *The Shining* a very average score: 61%. Of the ten reviews indexed by the site, only six give the movie over 60%. The *metascores* go from a measly 38 (given by the critic Jay Scott of the *Globe and Mail* in Toronto) to a perfect score (from the very enthusiastic Ian Nathan of *Empire*). More measured, the famed movie critic Roger Ebert gave it an 88%. Like every other Stanley Kubrick release, the critics were divided.

"Kubrick certainly doesn't fail small. One could fast forget *The Shining* as an overreaching, multi-levelled botch were it not for Jack Nicholson. Nicholson, one of the few actors capable of getting the audience to love him no matter what he does, is an ideal vehicle for Kubrick[1]."

Little by little, positive word of mouth gave the movie a semblance of commercial success. While *The Shining* attracted enough viewers to allow Warner Brothers to turn a modest profit, there's no doubt the critics weren't partic-

---

1. Review by Jay Scott, *The Globe and Mail*, June 14 1980, E1.

ularly kind to it. Stanley Kubrick and Jack Nicholson were even accused of having made a mess of a great book by expunging all the horror-movie potential out of the Stephen King novel which inspired the movie.

Stalyne Kubrick

Early December 1971. *A Clockwork Orange* was about to be released. Stanley Kubrick left nothing to chance, even though he lived in London. He learned that one of the New York movie theatres supposed to show his new movie had its walls and ceilings covered in white lacquer. Kubrick demanded the ceiling be repainted before his showing, in order to ensure there'd be no harsh glare. The theatre's owner doubted the work could be done in time for the release, slated for December 19.

Naturally obstinate, Kubrick wasn't the sort of man to back down from a fight. Still in England, he went through the Manhattan phone book, made a list of contractors able to set up the scaffolding and repaint the room. He dispatched the list to the movie theatre's owner. A few days later, a suspicious Kubrick decided to check in on the paint's finish: it was, as he feared, a glossy black, which would cause the same glare as the white paint. And so, under Kubrick's orders, the whole room was repainted again. A matte black was applied while the director, finally reassured, sat in his deep armchair on the other side of the Atlantic, sharing a pot of tea with his wife, Christiane. In Manhattan, *A Clockwork Orange* could finally be projected in optimal conditions.

* * *

"How was it, working with Kubrick?" Roger Ebert asked Shelley Duvall, some ten years after her work on *The Shining*.

"Almost unbearable," she admitted. "Going through day after day of excruciating work. Almost unbearable. Jack Nicholson's character had to be crazy and angry all the time. And in my character I had to cry twelve hours a day, all day long, the last nine months straight, five or six days a week[2]."

* * *

A particularly intense scene shows a close-up of the head chef, Dick Hallorann, having a vision of what's happening in the Overlook while watching television, lying on a bed in his room in Florida. The story goes that Stanley Kubrick made the actor go through the scene 160 times, despite the fact Scatman Crothers was an experienced hand at his trade (*One Flew Over the Cuckoo's Nest*, *The Twilight Zone*.) There is reason to question the filmmaker's motives. Why would he insist on so many takes of the same scene, of a man in a trance? Certainly Stanley Kubrick's reputation for perfectionism preceded him, but perhaps we should read in this maniacal, repetitive obsession a means to exasperate his actors, to force them to the edge of themselves into a fragile, brittle state. Just like the characters he was asking them to play.

And what if the real madman was Stanley Kubrick himself?

* * *

---

2. Translator's Note : Source, which doesn't appear in the original French, is: http://www.rogerebert.com/interviews/interview-with-shelley-duvall

A writer in his creative process becomes obsessed with a singular idea. Monomaniac, barely adjusted to society. And that's on his good days.

We can read *The Shining* as a dark fable on the creative process. Let us consider a writer, a father, waiting, full of guilt, for his children to go to bed in order to find refuge in his office, turn on his laptop, and get back to writing. He keeps only his best ideas, which come to him furtively: a flash here or there, while his hands are handcuffed to the car steering wheel or while he's in the shower. He becomes more and more distracted when someone talks to him. And his passion starts to devour him as the project moves forward, as he realizes that the chaos he was at first trying to modestly tame is beginning to take a coherent shape. How many acknowledgements and thanks does it take at the end of the book to feel less guilty about having dived deeply into yourself until you emerge, exhausted, with a completed work?

Stanley Kubrick, who considered every one of his projects carefully, who wrote and sketched and stained notebooks well before filming was to start, must be considered as a member of this strange tribe. A tribe almost like those diagnosed with OCD (obsessive-compulsive disorder). In days past, those who suffered from the illness were deemed to suffer from *obsessional neurosis*. They were neurotics, in other words. Well, well.

Now, we prefer a euphemistic term: OCD. Among the various types of OCDs, there's a particularly interesting category: those related to order, to tidying, to *symmetry*. Kubrick in a nutshell. A constant knocking, rattling in his mind. Knock, knock! "Wendy, I'm home!"

Forty-two cars are aligned in the Overlook parking lot at

the beginning of the movie, when Jack Torrance arrives for his interview.

As she backtracks up the stairs in the Colorado Lounge, Wendy swings at Jack with her baseball bat forty-two times.

Kubrick's obsession with the number 42 might well come from the Bible. Matthew in chapter 1, verses 1 to 17, tells of the forty-two generations of begetting between Jesus and the patriarch Abraham. A long enumeration, a genealogical tree. You might be tempted to think that the accountant apostle (a former tax collector; consequently good with numbers) was paid by the word.

Among the symptoms of OCD, there's *counting*, a mania for counting everything and anything, of touching an object a certain number of times, odd or even, of avoiding walking on lines, the cracks in a sidewalk, for example. Among the symptoms of OCD, there's a fear of having OCD, which can ironically trigger OCD. There are some who clearly count themselves senseless. Who can count on themselves being unfortunate.

Filter Film

Can a teacher actually maintain an interest in teaching the same work over and over again without it echoing something deep within him, some true emotion? Why study one movie over another? Why return to it year after year, semester after semester? It must because it embodies something, an intimate feeling, a passionate link, an obsessive one, even, between teacher and object. What would be the point, otherwise?

Sainte-Beuve introduced us to the idea of *biographical criticism*, in which the scholar lays the foundation of his analysis on biographical elements of the author's life. In such an analysis, it's necessary to know both the broad brushstrokes as well as the details of Balzac's life if we are to think about *The Quest of the Absolute* or *Cousin Bette*. After all, *I* isn't necessarily the other. Is there a parallel in education? A sort of *biographical pedagogy*, a form of subtle egotism that would make the teacher speak of himself through the text or film he asks his students to consider? The examination of a work is inevitably put through the sieve of the pedagogue's conscience. He is the one who decides it to be a valid object of study. We could even extrapolate: a work may affect, even shape, certain aspects of a reader's personality. This must be doubly true for the scholars who develop a continuous and deep relationship with a limited number of cultural artifacts. Like a long, insidious contamination. As the professor stands in front of his students, professing, he strives in good faith to contaminate them.

I must have watched *The Shining* at least forty times. I was ten years old at my first contact with *The Shining*. *"How'd you like some ice cream, Doc?"* I watched it a few more times: simple curiosity. Then more regularly as a teacher. A little bit OCD myself, I like to pretend I've seen the movie forty-two times, even if I know it has to be more than that by now. Like a certainty that slowly takes shape, I realize that the interest shared by my students and myself for this excellent movie can't be the only reason I systematically put Stanley Kubrick's film in my syllabus. By now, weariness for his work would have overwhelmed me, was it not for the fact that *The Shining* contains the tragic signs of the flaw within me.

I have never felt weariness, the opposite actually: it's as if careful study of Kubrick's movie allows me to slyly digest the darker elements of my macabre genealogy. It's as if I can see, in the labyrinthine corridors of the Overlook Hotel, the ghostly silhouettes of my family's past. Watching *The Shining* over and over again is no chore. No, it is a way of domesticating horror, to find in the homicidal script the possibility of a happy ending—in the Stanley Kubrick film just as in the Stephen King book from which it drew inspiration, the mother and son both escape, *in extremis,* the axe blows of a murderous Jack Torrance.

Watch, analyze, watch again, overanalyze: my deep examination of this magisterial work is akin to spooling out a thread behind me, like Ariadne. If I follow it through the oppressive maze of the Overlook Hotel, I'll escape, safe and sound, the frothing beast that's been chasing us, my mother and I, since 1942. Like little Danny who finds his way out of the green maze by retracing his steps, I can, guided by the terrifying lessons of *The Shining*, look back on a painful past and find the way out, towards the light. To find my own path out of the mire.

To make suffering aesthetic is to avoid looking horror directly in its eye. Sieve, decant, filter. And, like Danny Torrance, use all my cunning. To make suffering aesthetic is to repel its deadly impact by placing between real horror and my tormented mind a 140-minute movie. Make it absorb the hardest blows. If only Mom could have found refuge in a protective book or movie instead of letting herself be swarmed by the vigorous ivy of her terrible past. Who knows? Perhaps the metastasis on her soul would not have spread with the same intent.

Contrary to my mother, I can never lose my thread. My only happy ending is to march obstinately towards the light. To learn to walk with open wounds. I don't have a choice: I must let the rays of the sun rain down upon me like the chapter and verse from an irradiant sky of a magnificent Kubrick red.

The Mountain

Martin Scorsese, the filmmaker, wrote: "Watching a Kubrick film is like gazing up at a mountain top. You look up and wonder, 'How could anyone have climbed that high?'"

On the road from Boulder to Silver Lake, Colorado, if you look south, you can see Twin Sisters Peak.

Five days before the release of *The Shining*, the whole world discovered the mountains of America's Pacific Northwest, where some of the film's scenes were shot. On May 18, 1980, the eruption of Mount St. Helens became the most destructive in American history, outside of Alaska. When the president of the United States, Jimmy Carter, flew in to witness the extent of the destruction, he could only say, his face drawn, that the scene looked like a moonscape. Fifty-seven victims. Without mentioning the material damage: 200 homes, 47 bridges, 24 kilometres of railroad, and 300 kilometres of road were destroyed. And we can certainly have a thought for the area's wildlife as well.

On May 23, 1980, the day *The Shining* was released, a film crew landed on Mount St. Helens to shoot images of the destruction. Their compass needles went haywire, turned ceaselessly, and the documentarians were quickly lost. On May 24, a second eruption almost killed them. They'd be rescued two days later.

It's a three-and-a-half-hour drive to Mount St. Helens from Mount Hood, where some of *The Shining*'s exterior scenes were shot.

Black Screen

February 2013. Lanaudière regional hospital in Joliette. I walked by the nurses' station in the intensive care unit, smiling at the kind lady on duty there, the one with the round glasses, the same nurse as last time. I stopped in front of the room where my mother rested and backed up a step; an attendant had just finished changing the bed, placing the soiled sheets she'd bunched in an imperfect ball into a rolling hamper. She told me she'd be done in five minutes, and I could visit mom after that. I walked back to the nurses' station to grab a vase and placed the flowers I'd brought with me in it. I picked out two daisies and gave them to the nurse with the round glasses. After all, it was Valentine's Day, right?

"Thank you, Mr. Forest, you're very kind."

"Roy, Roy is my name. I've got my father's name."

"Oh! Of course. And you told me last time, didn't you? I'm sorry, Mr. Roy. I'm a bit of a scatterbrain when it comes to names."

She said she was touched by the flowers. "Thank you very much—I love daisies!" She took her glasses off and smiled.

Just then the orderly finally stepped out of my mother's room, and went on with her rounds.

I glanced through the door into her tiny room. I watched the woman lying in a raised bed. A thought crossed my mind: my life started in this now ruined body, a little over four decades ago. My mother was full of tubes, but didn't know why. Her eyes as she watched me enter were those of a wild beast, perhaps tracked by the very man who was here now, holding the flowers. Did she recognize me? As I aged, was I beginning to look, a little bit more every day, like her father, Jacques? I carefully made my way towards her bed, not wanting to startle her. I showed her the daisies I bought at the hospital florist on the ground floor. Her glazed-over eyes, misty with infinite distress, were those of a woman coming back from too-distant a place.

I placed the flowers in the vase still filled with the roses I brought last time.

"Hey, mom. I came yesterday, but you were sleeping," I said, loud enough for my voice to reach her, loud enough to break through the wall of her semi-comatose apathy. "I brought flowers. Daisies. Your favourite."

I didn't think it was worth telling her I'd been coming every day since she was admitted, on February 12. The antidote to the poison she swallowed left her in a state more lethargic than somnolent. But she seemed in better shape than forty-eight hours before, at least, when she was groaning, her breath short, mouth open, face sallow, completely unrecognizable. She still couldn't turn her head, so I moved into her field of vision. I stroked her grey hair while, with my other hand, I held onto her fingers tenderly.

"In a few weeks, mom, when it's summer out, if you're okay with it, we'll go out to Renaud Park. There are benches there, and we can watch the Assumption River go by, you remember? On our way there, we'll go buy a snack or something, everything we need to spend a few hours eating and chatting outside, barefoot in the grass. And we'll eat ripe red raspberries, just like we used to when I was small, do you remember? Just the two of us. And we'll look up towards the blue sky and I'll ask you to find a cloud that looks like a horse, or a turtle, or the head of a beagle even. Hold on, mom. In a few weeks, the snow will melt, we'll go to Renaud Park and watch the river go by. And the clouds."

I wasn't telling myself any lies, though. The prognosis was bleak. I said the words as a gift of softness, a breath of comfort. And if she couldn't hear me, perhaps at least she could feel the warmth of my hands. I picked up a cotton bud, dipped it into a jar of glycerin on her bedside table, and wet her dried lips and the inside of her mouth. Did the nurses remember to hydrate her with the glycerin when I wasn't there, when mom was left to herself?

The small card the florist gave me with the bouquet of daisies was blank, I didn't think it useful to write the usual words of encouragement: *get well soon!*

A Mad Idea

Breaking off from his habit of setting the plot of his novels in Castle Rock, Maine, Stephen King decided to force himself out of his comfort zone. The choice of his next destination was a product of chance: he placed his finger on a map of the United States at random. And so, not long after, the writer's family moved to Boulder, Colorado. During this temporary exile, Stephen King and his tribe spent time at the neoclassical Stanley Hotel (in the mountains of Estes Park). As charming as the place was, the family spent only a night...the establishment was almost deserted and scheduled to close the following day for a prolonged period.

The Stanley Hotel was inaugurated on July 4, 1909, by its owner, Freelan Oscar Stanley. About the hotel, mysterious anecdotes abound. Employees and guests have, over the years, reported similar stories as King did during his now famous stay in room 237. During his night in the room, Stephen King had a nightmare he wouldn't soon forget: his son, then aged three, running, terrorized, in the corridors of the Stanley Hotel, chased by a fire hose.

Back in Boulder, King attacked his typewriter like a madman: the first draft of *The Shining* was ready in four months.

The story goes that the Stanley Hotel is haunted: kitchen employees claim they sometimes hear sounds of celebration coming from the ballroom. When they go to check on it, they find it empty every time.

Others say they hear the tinkling of a piano in the same ballroom, despite it being empty. What's more, or so it's said, the late-lamented wife of the owner and founder of the hotel, Ms. Flora Stanley, enjoyed playing the piano.

Other witnesses speak of a ghost, standing mutely at the foot of their bed in the middle of the night, before, without warning, winking out of existence once more.

The Stanley Hotel's management didn't seem to hold Stanley Kubrick's decision to shoot the movie in another hotel in Oregon, the Timberline Lodge, and in the studios in Elstree, England, against him. After all, *The Shining* has played on a loop in every one of the hotel's rooms for years. On channel 42, of course. Some things go without saying.

I hope I get to spend a night at the Timberline Lodge one day, even more than in the Stanley Hotel. I would be somewhere on Mount Hood. The lodge is a ritzy hotel in the snowy heights of Oregon. I hope I'd dream good dreams there. Because it's on Mount Hood—and not in Colorado—that some of the exterior scenes of Kubrick's movie were shot.

* * *

Stephen King published *The Shining* at the beginning of 1977, barely a year before Kubrick began filming, on May 1, 1978. I should mention John Calley's role in this whole affair. He was a producer at Warner Brothers. He was the one who came up with the idea of sending Stanley Kubrick a draft version of Stephen King's book, while it was still an unfinished manuscript.

Shooting ended in April 1979. It was released on May 23, 1980.

Stanley Kubrick's adaptation of the movie took roads left untrammeled by the novel. Stephen King refused to have his name appear in the movie's credits. It should be said that the director ignored a number of themes and ideas present in the novel to make the story his own. More than a simple ghost story, more than a disguised confession of the ravages of alcoholism, Kubrick made the words of the original King novel into an exploration of madness and its potentially murderous consequences.

The Mirror

How many hours can a man avoid seeing his reflection in a mirror? How many times a day does he have an opportunity to see himself in a mirror, in a storefront, in a spoon, in the darkened screen of a television set, in a rear-view mirror, in the eyes of someone he loves, in his iPhone, or in the reflection in a pond?

Mirrors don't lie. *Mirror, mirror on the wall, who's the fairest one of all?*

> The queen thought that she was again the most beautiful woman in the land, and the next morning she stepped before the mirror. The mirror answered:
>
> "You, my queen, are fair; it is true. But Little Snow White beyond the seven mountains is a thousand times fairer than you."
>
> It startled the queen to hear this, and she knew that she had been deceived, that the huntsman had not killed Snow White.

And what if the truth about Jack and Danny Torrance was hidden within the mirror's reflection?

* * *

It is universally known that children love striking terror in the hearts of their slightly younger peers. In Saint-Alexis, my neighbour, Daniel Landry, was no exception.

He challenged the kids on my street, aged between six and ten, to do a special ritual that would make the devil's image appear right before our eyes. We were to follow three steps: first, we had to gaze skywards and count twelve stars in the night sky (not to be confused with the blinking lights of a passing plane); then, we had to run around our houses twelve times in a row, without stopping; finally, we had to stare at our reflection in the bathroom mirror for twelve seconds (one Mississippi, two Mississippi, three Mississippi ... twelve...) without blinking a single time. The terrible image should appear, a red-faced devil superimposed on our own faces. Goat's horns and pitchfork not included.

I counted to twelve more than once, staring at the bathroom mirror, to no avail. Only my round freckled face and my Danny Torrance haircut filled the mirror.

When I think back to it, I'm surprised I became so committed to the game. After all, as far back as I can remember, I've always felt a vague unease at watching myself in a mirror, as if staring at myself, looking into my own eyes, would lead to a hallucinatory deformation, a slow change, a pixelization of my own face. As if I was melting. An interpenetration whose inevitable conclusion was the destruction of my being. As if the reflected image would crush the real one, swallow it whole.

* * *

What could be more natural than to study the idea of the double when your first name is a palindrome? The psychoanalyst Otto Rank had a rather peculiar point of view on mirrors. He perceived them as doors opening onto the soul. Sometimes, I think that what makes intimacy with my double so clearly intolerable to me is the fear of what I might discover on the other side.

Jacques Lacan published an essay in 1970 called *The Mirror Stage as Formative of the I Function*. Lacan believed that, between the ages of six and eighteen months, the child goes through a crucial developmental stage. We've all witnessed a young child approaching a mirror, where he sees his image reflected. Inevitably, he'll attempt to touch it or even look behind the mirror, trying to discover what might be hidden. At some point, he'll realize that he's seeing a simple image, and will no longer be fascinated by what is behind the mirror. He knows there is nothing to find. Finally, he'll realize that the image he's staring at is his own, and will recognize himself in it. From then on, he'll begin to have an awareness of his own personhood. As if the mirror was a necessary implement in the structuring of his own identity. And so it goes in *The Shining*.

When he makes his way to the ballroom to have a bourbon and confide in Lloyd, the barman, Jack Torrance takes the corridor leading to the Gold Room. He's suddenly wracked by convulsions, his whole body shaking, the spasms of a madman. But they only occur when he passes by the mirrors suspended along the wall to his right. There are four mirrors; four times he gesticulates wildly, a spectacular lunatic.

* * *

While researching his adaptation of the Stephen King

novel, Stanley Kubrick and Diane Johnson, an academic specializing in gothic novels with whom Kubrick wrote *The Shining*'s script, dove deep into one of Freud's essays, "Das Unheimliche," exploring the concept of the uncanny. The director's main objective was to create a movie whose aesthetic and structure would be guided by the Austrian doctor's essay.

To do so, Kubrick multiplied the references to the theme of the double, mirrors, scenes echoing each other, and the repression of impulses in various forms. The scene in which Jack Torrance admits to his wife, Wendy, that he feels good at the Overlook, better than he's ever felt, is part of this theme. After all, he claims to be able to intuitively feel what is around every corner of the hotel's corridors. The impressions of *déjà vu* are felt to the extreme, as if Jack is stuck in an inescapable, hidden system of recurrences and correspondences. A consenting captive of a gigantic spatiotemporal maze. Condemned to repeat the same gestures, events, the same crimes, Jack Torrance *is* Charles Grady, Jack Torrance *is* Delbert Grady, Jack Torrance *is* that smiling man in the picture dated 1921, a picture taken during the Independence Day ball.

Heinrich Ludwig Kleyer

The German industrialist Heinrich Ludwig Kleyer succeeded in business thanks to the mass production of cars, motorbikes, and bicycles, as well as office furniture, typewriters and even tricycles. Right until the company he'd founded in Frankfurt, Germany in 1880, *Adlerwerke vorm, Heinrich Kleyer AG* was taken over in 1957 by Grundig, a company headquartered in Nuremburg. Adler's well-known symbol was an homage to Imperial Germany's heraldry, the famous black eagle in a triumphant pose. *Natüralich*, if one knows that Adler means "eagle" in English.

Without seeking to establish a causal link, it is interesting nonetheless to know that, during the Second World War, the Nazi Ministry of Aviation published in Berlin an illustrated bimonthly magazine whose title was simply *Adler*.

* * *

Noise—a bombardment perhaps—in a hotel's décor. The regularity of it is intriguing. Twelve hard knocks heard coming from a source outside the frame while the spectator sees a close-up of an ancient, nearly extinct typewriter during *The Shining*'s filming, towards the end of the 1970s. The director likely had a very particular reason for showing the typewriter with a blank page inserted, in the middle of the frame. A German typewriter, the terrifying Adler.

The framing is perfectly symmetrical. To signal artistic impotence, the Adler is flanked by an ashtray in which a single cigarette, recently lit, is burning itself out. A Marlboro, if the open pack is a clue. A few pens and pencils complete the tableau. The page wrapped in the typewriter's cylinder is immaculate.

The shooting script, annotated by Stanley Kubrick, features, at scene forty-eight, a single hand-written phrase, as evasive as it is laconic: "Jack is not working." As vague as it was, the director made the choice of not specifying what his leading actor should be doing. Almost the opposite of stage direction. Instead, what he is supposed to *not* be doing is underlined. How does one act as if one is *not working*? How to illustrate the idleness of a lazy writer procrastinating? Jack Torrance's performer, Nicholson himself, came up with the idea, which would become iconic. He bounced a yellow tennis ball around the abandoned hotel. The bombardment wasn't one, after all. At least not strictly speaking.

* * *

During the darker days of the Shoah, the Nazis responsible for writing down the names of Jews on their fateful lists hammered away, like so many ghastly impacts, on the keys of a Berchtesgaden Adler. White keys, cloth ink ribbon, unicolor, twenty-five millimetres wide. Mindless bureaucracy at the service of the most rigorous murderous efficiency. The incessant slapping of those keys must have alienated even the most lucid minds. The beauty of mechanical precision wielded as an instrument of systematic persecution.

We could be forgiven for thinking that, more than solitude, more than isolation, the cadenced hammering of the grey Adler's keys made the failed writer Jack Torrance completely mad.

"The only thing that can get a bit trying up here during the winter is the tremendous sense of isolation," Stuart Ullman, the hotel's manager warns, resigned at having to move onto the slippery slope of morbid confidences.

"Well, that just happens to be exactly what I'm looking for. I'm outlining a new writing project, and five months of peace is just what I want," Jack answers, enthusiastic despite the warning.

In the end, the self-described author Jack Torrance will manage to write nothing but hundreds of insane pages of the same phrase, spat onto every one, *ad nauseam*: "All work and no play makes Jack a dull boy."

Winter, a deserted hotel, a spider spins its web on the Overlook's ceiling, the mad writer bangs and bangs and bangs on the keys of his Nazi-grey Adler.

To Overlook

To Overlook. *Verb; to ignore, to condone, to turn a blind eye.*
Overlook. *Noun; a place from which to look down upon a scene.*

* * *

Twelve hard knocks tear through a silence as deep as the grave. Twelve hard knocks ringing off a Navajo tapestry suspended on one of the Colorado Lounge's walls. A determined-looking Jack Torrance stands before it. We can guess symmetric patterns of slender silhouettes, standing straight. Among them, two spindly azure figures. As the shot progresses—a shot where words are unnecessary—references to the Native American genocide are mixed in with allusions to the Holocaust under the empty gaze of a bison whose stuffed head observes the scene of symbolic destruction from on high.

The North American bison seems to be witnessing the sad spectacle of history repeating itself. A *déjà vu*, like we are witness to so often in this haunted hotel, the aptly named Overlook. And the ashes of the Marlboro left burning, staining the ashtray to the right of the typewriter, as indifferent as a Pole in 1942.

* * *

During the Second World War, the industrialist Heinrich Ludwig Kleyer was forced to follow the Nazi regime's orders and contribute to the war effort by producing military vehicles. The Nazi emblem was nearly identical to Adler's. The wheel on which Adler's eagle lay was swapped out for a swastika. Adler thus became the patented image of a massacre of historical proportions. Never were such quantities of ash seen, be they on the ground or falling from the sky like soft snow sullied by an apocalypse.

Trauma

The word *traumatism* comes from the Greek τραῦμα (trauma) meaning *wound, damage*. Those having suffered psychological trauma have a tendency to repeatedly relive the pain they underwent, through the sensations and perceptions that the traumatic event initially created, despite whatever efforts are made to avoid the sources of their repeated flashbacks.

She soiled her bed for a long time. Two, three times a week. She suffered from nocturnal enuresis until an abnormally late age. Thirteen, fourteen years old. In the small child's room she shared with her twin sister, she'd wake up, panting, her cheeks moist, her face wet with salty tears. Her pajamas wet, imbibed with warm urine. For having known it as children, we all remember that uncomfortable feeling.

Abruptly awoken by the cries coming from the room next door, her grandmother would get out of bed, its springs creaking. She would bring her to the bathroom to summarily clean her in the darkness of night. The harsh scratching of the washcloth. The relief at putting on dry clothes. Instead of changing the soiled sheets for new ones, her grandmother invited her to slip under her own warm sheets to finish the night. The smell of lilac on the pillow. Soft comfort. Now the odd man out, grandpa would be immediately kicked out of bed to finish the night on the uncomfortable living room couch.

At the same time, as a child, she had terrible nightmares. She would howl in terror. Imagined terror, seemingly so real when she woke. Her mother physically assaulted by a man, who, in her dreams, wasn't her father. The bastard fixed her with the kindest smile playing on his lips as he beat her mom. She couldn't stop staring at his cruelly affable smile. Flattened on the kitchen table, her mother's smooth features were now torn to shreds. It was of unconscionable violence. She never told the exact plot of her nightmares to her grandmother. She would have worried too much.

* * *

Solitude is dangerous. Over a prolonged period, it forces a person to face himself, to meditate on his destiny, on his fate. If the individual in question has nihilistic tendencies, solitude can lead him into the abyss of desperate thoughts.

Her hand was tepid. Not warm, not cold, reminding me that she vegetated somewhere between life and death. She blinked, occasionally. Her face was without expression when I spoke to her. Her absence of reaction didn't make me lose hope now. Can grieving begin before death?

As we grow older, the relationship with our parents changes, as if the roles finally invert themselves. The child slowly, progressively, takes on the parental role; he begins, with time, to support his own parents in a way. Meanwhile, the mother regresses with age and declining health until she becomes a vulnerable little girl you need to reassure in times of crisis.

I just wanted to be next to her. I continued to stroke her hair, talking about her granddaughter, Aurore, looking in her eyes for a light, a spark, a sign of acknowledgement that would not come. Anything, really, some sort of sign of well-being, of peace. Anything but this glacial emptiness. What I would have given to be able to bore a hole into her conscience. *Everything will be okay, mom. Everything will be okay. We'll do as you wish. We won't be unnecessarily stubborn; I'll make sure of it.*

The path towards awakening something takes the most improbable turns. Swallowing all of her antidepressants on the evening of February 11, she wanted to put an end to the nightmares that tortured her nights and, in the same fell blow, put an end to an existence made of the stuff of torment and obsession. Her mind was like a blackboard, the anxiolytics the eraser. Raw despair.

Through the tubes that connected her to life, she didn't smile when I told her that my little Aurore wrote a love poem to Thomas, the neighbour who sits next to her on the school bus. I wondered, in my head: *Did you write love poems when you were seven, mom? Was there room in your life for love after what you went through?*

I held her hand softly, applying tender pressure on her lukewarm, wrinkled fingers. I knew very well I was a thousand leagues away.

Red Rum

I t is profoundly pointless to try to make a river run backwards, to make it climb back to its source.

By dint of attempting to reveal the successive layers of this hidden past, I came to learn two things: one, memory works in frustrating fits and starts, and two, my family wasn't true level, as if twisted by a distant flaw transmitted from generation to generation.

My maternal grandfather, Jacques Forest, came from an Acadian family who received land in order to settle Montcalm County, at most some one hundred kilometres from Montreal, in the middle of the nineteenth century. Big families weren't rare back then, and so the descendants of the first Forest who came to the region dispersed through the small agricultural communities around the Village de l'Industrie (now called Joliette), like Saint-Alexis, Saint-Jacques, Saint-Esprit, Sainte-Julienne, Sainte-Marie-Salomé, Saint-Liguori.

His mother's death, Jeanne was her name, in the middle of the 1910s, precipitated things for young Jacques. Since he didn't get along with his stepmother, the child was placed, at only seven years old, with a neighbour, a farmer by the name of Stanislas Dupuis, who owned a rather large and prosperous farm, and was a part-time moonshine whisky distiller. Jacques' contact with his father, Daniel, and his brothers became increasingly rare, until his father died, three years later, from sepsis, a consequence of an infected broken toe suffered after having given a mighty kick at his strongbox that he couldn't manage to open.

Young Jacques must have suffered immensely from the sense of emptiness caused by his parents' premature death. He would try to fill that emptiness, later, with rum and tall beers until he managed to kill himself with drink at the tender age of Christ.

Go tell a man who has cancer that alcoholism is a disease, just to see his reaction. Everything is a question of will and choice. Alcoholism is a weakness. To say the opposite is to speak in bad faith. You don't choose, for example, to have prostate cancer that tears at you from the inside. You suffer from it, that's all. A diagnostic-like a punch in the face. Like the boring injustice of blind fate.

I'm aware Stanley Kubrick was putting old wine in a new bottle when he resorted to a bottle of Jack Daniel's with two of his characters and actors being named Jack (Torrance/ Nicholson) and Danny (Torrance/Lloyd). Because it is indeed Lloyd, the ghostly bartender who serves Jack Daniel's to Jack Torrance when the latter says to himself in front of the bar mirror in the ballroom: "God, I'd give anything for a drink. My goddamn soul, just for a glass of beer."

I'm aware Stanley Kubrick was putting old wine in a new bottle knowing that scotch is often called "red rum" in the United States.

And I'm aware that I'm putting old wine in a new bottle when I use the image of wine and bottles one too many times in a chapter titled "red rum."

Once Upon a Time in the West

I try to think this world hasn't gone mad. Each day reveals a new reason to believe that nothing makes sense anymore.

Without a doubt one of Stanley Kubrick's richest and most complex movies, *The Shining,* has exerted unfailing fascination for more than thirty years. The obvious interest I've had in it is less related to a hidden mystery than a way of exorcizing my family's past, marked by a crime. That distant crime still echoes in our fragile Forest minds.

The last tremors of it were felt in the winter of 2013, when my mother was found cold, unconscious, in her bed in her modest apartment. The morning of February 12, 2013. The daughter of Jacques Forest and his wife Aurore (nee Pauzé) made an attempt to end her life by swallowing, on February 11, a large quantity of pills (Restoril, Seropram, Tylenol, Rivotril).

* * *

1942. Saint-Alexis-de-Montcalm. An empty dog dish in a shed. Affixed to the back wall, a strong rope slung over a dark beam, falling vertically on the other side, perpendicular to a small wooden bucket tipped to the ground. At the end of the rope, held up by a loop around his throat, a man hangs, rigid. His sky-blue shirt bloodied. Dr. Jacques Forest's face is terrifying.

It isn't only in movies that men kill their wives.

Exit Music (for a Film)

April 1984. The principal of my seminary in Joliette fetched me from my classroom, on the fifth floor. Not a word on the reason for the visit, but his contrite air augured nothing good. His sombre face led me to believe that he wouldn't want to be in my shoes. A policeman waited for me at the school's entrance.

How is it that I still hear that crushing silence so many years later? I was in the back of his unmarked car. His eyes making an effort to avoid mine in the rear-view mirror. The cop refused to explain (likely because he was prohibited from doing so) the reasons behind this unusual ride.

* * *

To rip out the stitches from a past you believe you left behind. The day her existence crumbled announced the day she would exit her life for good. The interval between those two moments would reveal itself to be nothing more than a long reprieve. My life centred on my search for a woman who, her whole life, sought death. My mother tried to kill herself for the first time in April 1984. It took forty-two years for her cup to run over for the first time.

She was found earlier that day, just in time, in her bed. Dozens of open pill bottles on the bedside table. I spent two days in the waiting room of the intensive care unit where a medical team was trying to keep Danielle Forest alive. My visits to the room were brief. Seeing my mother stuck with tubes at such a young age—I wasn't yet sixteen—surrounded by all sorts of blinking equipment, hearing her laboured breathing echoing in her oxygen mask. It all traumatized me.

My mother got better after a few months in the psychiatric wing of the regional hospital on Boulevard Sainte-Anne, in Joliette.

I know it's strange, but I remember one thing above all about that dark period in my adolescence. A side effect of her stomach being pumped was that my mother's voice changed slightly. Each subsequent conversation, each phone call, brought me back to her gesture of distress and desertion, that day in April 1984. An indelible mark of her failed suicide. Like an audible reminder that it had really happened. That it could happen again, at any time.

That gravely note in her voice was far from the most serious consequence of her action, since she suffered from chronic depression until her very last moments. Yes, you can save someone from physical death, you can make them better and sign off on their good health, release them from a mental ward, but you can't force life back into them, can't give them the strength to live. That spark, the one spoken of in the mysteries, can't be transmitted by injections or pills. Forget the saline solutions and the syringes, you can't force-feed someone with the desire to live.

The Big Fluker

I never believed I had a gift, even if I became a sort of circus attraction in high school thanks to my preternatural ability to always guess correctly when asked what grade one of my classmates had gotten on an exam a teacher just returned to us. I always put these "predictions" on the back of pure instinct. In truth, I didn't really have a secret. Simply, as soon as the question was asked, I spontaneously burst out with the first number that came to mind. Nine times out of ten I got it right, always to the amused stupefaction of my audience, even if we all agreed it was fluke, pure luck. But luck repeated over and over again is never banal. My classmates would say I was the luckiest, the flukiest, and they gave me the nickname The Big Fluker in a fit of quickly dissipated enthusiasm as we all turned to more serious things, like trying to solve the six sides of a Rubik's cube. An exercise I was far less successful at.

I never really believed I had a gift, despite that one time at the Silhouette Club, a bar in Hull (an industrial town in North Eastern England) in the early 90s. My German friend Ute and I had one after the other guessed (should I say *anticipated*?) the title of four consecutive songs the DJ was about to play. The memory of this episode is still strong in both our minds: "There is a Light That Never Goes Out" (The Smiths), "Disintegration" (The Cure), "The Saturday Boy" (Billy Brag) and "Ceremony" (New Order)... Towards the end of the current song, both of us tried to predict the following one. Four times we told the other to guess, and four times we got it right. In my case, the two times I had to guess a title, I respected a rule I had given myself: not to think and spontaneously blurt out the first title among the many that crowded my mind. Wanting to end our challenge on a positive note, we agreed to stop, equally fascinated and worried by what was occurring. We never dared play our game again.

I never actually believed I had gift, even though I defied all predictions and managed to get a seat among the team of four smart kids who would be representing the Joliette Seminary on *Génies en Herbe*, a nationally televised quiz show for high school students. During the auditions, three of the four roles were already filled when my friends encouraged me to step up to the plate on a laugh. I was to measure up against a talented girl, on a Wednesday over lunch. Having nothing to lose and being rather motivated at the prospect of being able to skip classes during travels to intercollegiate competitions, I frenetically pressed the button as soon as the first words of every question were uttered. It was as if I had the supernatural ability to read through the cardboard question slips Miss Marsolais, the teacher responsible for asking the questions, held. I answered correctly and rapidly as three other members who'd already made the team looked on, amused, along with a few friends who'd come to support me.

"What insec…"

"Butterfly!"

"Right. What year did the insurrect…"

"1837!"

"Yes. Who played for the Calgary Flam…"

"Joel Otto!"

"Right again, Mr. Roy."

The straight faces of the other members of the staff responsible for the activity betrayed their displeasure. They likely found my attitude too carefree, toeing the line of arrogance, going against the grain of the respect we were supposed to demonstrate for this sort of essential intellectual activity. But I continued breathlessly, inspired by some sort of demonic energy, feeling no pressure whatsoever. I was building up what would soon be the unshakable conviction that I would win, easily, handily.

A little like those feverish players who lose all ability to think clearly between two winning bets at the casino, convinced with stubborn certainty that they were, that night, blessed by the gods of roulette, nothing stopped me until the final bell rang, signaling the end of the memorable duel. It would remain in the annals of the Joliette Seminary. A crushing defeat, 410 to 170, inflicted by The Big Fluker. It could be argued that my victory was convincing. But I knew how to put things in perspective; if I'd played that same game the next day or a year later, the result would surely have been the opposite.

But over lunch that day, I could feel—no, I could *know*—the questions before they were even spoken. A state of grace, of inexplicable elevation, a communion with something vaster than myself.

The decisive nature of what had to be called a convincing victory didn't leave the teachers in charge of the group's composition much of a choice. I would proudly represent the Joliette Seminary during the taping of *Génies en Herbe*.

After a faultless run, our school won the national final against Laval College. Despite an honest contribution by

The Big Fluker to the team's success (I was the specialist on questions pertaining to sports and languages), it was the name of my opponent of that fateful lunchtime confrontation that was engraved in the commemorative cup given to the winners of the competition. She had the kindness, as a substitute, to come in for me at the last minute. During the final games (the semi-final and the final), I couldn't make it to Montreal for the taping in the Radio-Canada studios. My mother hadn't been able to resist the desperate impulse to swallow, that very same week, all her Celexa pills in her first suicide attempt. My place was definitely beside her in the intensive care unit instead of on a television set playing the Counting Horse with well-combed geniuses, bow ties and all.

Il Grande Massacro

Some of those who've analyzed *The Shining* see in the torrents of Kubrick-red blood pouring out of the doors of the Overlook Hotel's elevator a symbol for mass murder. True to himself, Kubrick never settled the issue definitively.

We can speculate that all this blood is that of Native Americans, bled bone dry by encroaching settlers. Native Americans were so systematically annihilated that only terms like genocide or mass murder can do justice to their experience. Stuart Ullman, the hotel's director, while leading the visiting Torrances on a tour around the hotel grounds, mentions that the establishment was built between 1907 and 1909. Supposedly on an Indian burial ground, the builders "actually had to repel a few Indian attacks while building it."

* * *

In 1889, William Monroe Wright founded the Calumet Baking Powder Company in Chicago whose logo, appearing on boxes of chemical yeast, shows the head of a tribal chief. The logo reminds us of similar imagery like the emblem of Chicago's hockey club, the Blackhawks. In *The Shining*, Kubrick twice shows us the red Calumet chemical yeast box, placed strategically in the Overlook's pantry. Once right behind Dick Hallorann's head when he speaks the words which marked my childhood in that slow-motion voice: *"How'd you like some ice cream, Doc?"* The other time behind the head of Jack Torrance, locked by his wife in the refrigerated room after she cracks him over the head with a baseball bat.

In a scene where the head chef, Dick Hallorann, attempts to return to the hotel in a small snowcat, we get a shot of the actor Scatman Crothers in profile, tuque and hood over his head. His silhouette seems like an echo of the tribal chief on the Calumet chemical yeast tin. A parallel, then, between the fate the supposedly civilized white man helped engineer for both Native Americans and African Americans.

We killed the chief, the chef. We must be sensitive to every frame, every shot, if we are to notice all the internal allusions and echoes in a movie that weaves a web of coherence far beyond what is initially perceived. Jack Torrance throws his yellow tennis ball down the hotel corridor, against its floor, its walls. The exact spots where the ball bounces are calculated by Kubrick, foretelling a tragedy. A subterranean prophesy. We must be attentive to the accessories seemingly scattered around Jack: a Big Wheel tricycle, a plush black bear.

When Jack Torrance sinks his axe into chef Hallorann's heart after he quite uselessly comes to the rescue, the old man crumbles to the floor at the very spot where Jack, earlier, had bounced his damned yellow tennis ball.

The black plush toy abandoned in the hall is in the very same position as Hallorann, laid low by a fatal blow. Kubrick placed the toy where the old black man would later fall. Is it a coincidence that the bear wears a piece of Kubrick-red cloth?

The Forest Sisters

The late 1970s. My mother's birthday. She was turning forty, maybe a little more. No matter her exact age, since we were witnessing a recurring scene, one acted out on the same date, year after year. I didn't interrupt her; she wasn't naturally talkative.

She spoke for a good twenty minutes, telling me all about what it feels like to lose someone. Telling me about her sister's life, Christiane, she would have been forty that day, maybe a bit more. It was as if, by talking about her sister who'd disappeared, she gave herself the cruel luxury of sustaining expectations.

No one remembers the story today. Probably because they thought she was just another runaway. People disappear every day. Seventeen people a day in Quebec alone. Runaways, parental abductions, kidnappings.

Sometimes, the disappeared float back to the surface. Annihilated, they're found in some seedy motel after having lost everything at the blackjack table or the roulette wheel. They bet their existence—consequently their family's existence—on black instead of red.

Sometimes, you find them in some topless bar in the deepest fold of this freaking armpit universe, or on the sidewalk, under the sway of a pimp, forcing them to whore themselves out to pay back a drug debt, a gambling debt.

Other times, the disappeared simply vanish to find a new

life, to give themselves a fresh start with a guy with a full bank account or a woman half as young.

More often than not, you never find them again.

My mother's twin sister disappeared the year of their fourteenth birthday. The impact it had on her grandparents, who were her guardians, is easy to fathom. They kept a mask of contriteness until the day they died, twenty years later. A disappearance is an inexplicable void that even the relief of death can't fill.

Today is my mother's birthday. Danielle. She's no longer here, but I can still hear her talking about her sister, disappeared. And I don't interrupt her.

Perfect Kiss

Fall 1984 in Joliette. Mom's been back in the apartment for a dozen days. The hospital where she received psychiatric treatment released her. She went to bed particularly early that night, leaving me alone in the living room with a girl from my class, Catherine.

It was a quarter past eight and a tape of *Unknown Pleasures* was on its second play through. Thank god for auto reverse... Catherine and I were in our second hour of making out on the couch. Our hands moved over each other's bodies with rather sweet tenderness—and mounting frustration at our too-tight jeans. Her hand in my hair, she let herself be kissed on the neck. I bit her swollen lips tenderly. My hand brushed against the skin of her back, under her satin blouse. I didn't dare undo her bra. The next time, maybe, but not tonight. Her tongue...

Ian Curtis singing: "Where will it end?" Joy Division's music made the moment that much more intense. Anyway, I was in my own paradise, here, no way I would leave her arms, get up from the couch, walk three steps, and put on another tape. Come on! Keep the rhythm, Peter Hook, you've got me in the right groove. The warmth of her slender arms, the smell of her hair. Must she really be home by ten?

Above us, on the next floor up, an apathetic woman in her early forties was in her bedroom. My mother slept like the dead, knocked out more than numbed by Ativan. And I, the self-centered virgin, kissed a girl for the first time. Curtis moved to "New Dawn Fades" and I never felt so alive.

Heeeere's Johnny!

Any text is the absorption and transformation of another text, as the semiotician Julia Kristeva wrote. The same holds true for movies.

A mouse-grey fall Saturday. Rain is in the air. A perfect afternoon for cocooning, just my daughter and I. A moment of tenderness the way I like them. Popcorn bowl between my legs, the head of my Aurore resting against me, we watch a family movie on television, comfortably sinking into our couch. Aurore is too young to understand the real reason why I smile when the shark goes chasing after the clown fish in *Finding Nemo*. Breaking through a metallic door behind which Nemo and his ally Dory are hiding, Bruce the shark manages to slip his head through the door, shouting: "*Heeeere's* Bruceeeyyy!"

* * *

On September 29, 1980, the scene where Jack Torrance announces his threatening arrival after several axe blows on the door behind which his wife is hiding runs as the opening for the anniversary of the *Tonight Show*, broadcast on NBC.

Jack Nicholson improvised the line which later gained cult status. He found inspiration in Ed McMahon's formula —*Heeeere's* Johnny!—which announced, to the crowd's applause, Johnny Carson's arrival in the studio. The eighteenth year of Carson's tenure was being celebrated on September 29, 1980. Kubrick hesitated about that shot for the movie's final cut. In the end, he trusted Nicholson's intuition.

Back when he played Jack Torrance in *The Shining*, Nicholson was a volunteer firefighter. The famous scene in the bathroom as Jack tears through the door with his axe, a door protecting a frenzied and vulnerable Wendy, took three days of filming and some sixty doors. The firefighter in Nicholson wanted to use a real axe.

* * *

To prepare for next week's class, I watch *Broken Blossoms*, a silent 1919 film by D.W. Griffith, starring Lillian Gish and Donald Crisp. The movie tells the story of a young girl, Lucy, suffering the repeated abuse of her alcoholic and violent father, Battling Burrows. In a scene from which Kubrick clearly drew inspiration, we see Battling Burrows use an axe to tear through the cupboard door in which young Lucy is hiding, terrorized.

While the sheer amount of intertextual scenes inspiring *The Shining* would be hard to count, there is value in searching for what came before, way back, as far back as silent film. Through this we can attempt to find the scene's origin. A 1921 movie by the Swede Victor Sjöström, *The Phantom Carriage* (*Körkarlen* is its original title), may prefigure even more precisely Jack breaking through the bathroom door with his axe, exclaiming: "*Heeeere's* Johnny!"

The Burns Sisters

Interior Hotel/Corridor M.S.[4]

Two little GRADY girls holding hands. (From scene 14 of *The Shining*)

* * *

There's something fascinating about identical twins. While we see them in a positive light, generally, there's something slightly strange in their relationship, nonetheless. The intimacy, the connivance, the silent communication, the unshakable bond, and that implicit feeling of superiority that being a twin provides. It's always intimidated me. Identical twins stand out for their rarity, their solidarity among a mosaic of deeply irreconcilable solitudes. No matter the challenges of life, a twin will always have the other, indefectible, to count on until death.

Their other self.

The soul mate.

Their other part.

The other, doubled.

---

4. *Daily Script, The Shining,* http://www.dailyscript.com/scripts/shining.html (visited July 9 2014). *The Shining*'s script uses a series of abbreviations. M.S. refers to *Medium Shot,* L.S. *Long Shot,* and M.C.S. *Medium Close-Up Shot.*

I think the most terrible inconvenience of having an identical twin is the macabre idea that must become an obsession as you grow older together: one day, one will see the other in a casket. And he'll think: I'm the one lying in that box. Beyond the loss of his alter ego, beyond the disappearance of his other self, it's the fact of seeing, in a sense, yourself dead that must make the experience absolutely traumatizing for the surviving twin.

* * *

In his youth, as a photographer for Look magazine, Stanley Kubrick studied photography beside the celebrated Diane Arbus, to whom we owe the intriguing picture "Identical Twins, Roselle, New Jersey, 1967." According to Kubrick's biographer, Patricia Bosworth, during the auditions for the Grady sisters—roles awarded to Lisa and Louise Burns— the filmmaker sought to reproduce the slight asymmetry found in the picture of the New Jersey twins.

There is a picture of the shoot floating around. We see the Burns sisters backstage, one walking behind the other, radiant smiles on their lips, followed by a woman filming them from behind the set decoration. A man I can't identify is seated to their right, wearing a suit. He watches them walk by, smiling. Even in this relaxed context, I can't help finding the Burns sisters inexplicably worrying. It's hard to guess from these picture alone that they were about to shoot the scene that would mark the imagination of all those who later watched the movie.

The Burns sisters never acted in another movie. Lisa has a degree in literature. Louise is a microbiologist.

Soon, Jack Torrance will wake from his nightmare, howling like a lunatic. Krzysztof Penderecki's serialism. *The Dream of Jacob*. A brilliant choice by Kubrick: even the title refers to Jack's tormented soul. The filmmaker loved music; and now, with this choice, he is foreshadowing the worst. Jack sees himself in his dream, chopping Wendy and Danny into pieces with an axe. As her husband begins barking himself awake, Wendy is in the Overlook's warm belly, attempting to get the furnace working in the boiler room.

The whole scene is made that much more compelling when you notice there's a black-and-white picture on a piece of furniture right next to the washing machine. By zooming in on the image, you can see—a shudder running down your spine—that it is indeed the two twin girls, identical and blond, holding each other by the hand. Take your magnifying glasses out: it's worth it.

* * *

Jack Torrance being interviewed in Stuart Ullman's office. In addition to the symmetrical framing, the furniture and accessories are placed in order to create a left/right equilibrium: the couches, plants, the window panes behind the director. Even the addition of another character, Watson, helps harmonize the scene by making him play the almost mute double of Jack in the balanced composition of the scene.

On the beige curtains framing the window panes, patterned letters: W, W. Double u (you), double u (you). Double, in German, is *Doppelgänger*. Since the nineteenth century, it has been one of the most popular themes in fantastic literature. From Edgar Allan Poe's **W**illiam **W**ilson to Stephen King's more recent texts, like *Secret* **W**indo**w,** the appearance of the double is often considered to be an ill omen.

By creating the tandem of Jekyll and Hyde in 1886, Robert Louis Stevenson predicted Freudian psychoanalytic theories by a few decades: his Mr. Hyde represents, in a sense, all the violent and perverse impulses of the good Dr. Jekyll.

So does Jack.

I Don't Like Mondays (Tell Me Why)

American rock stations used to play the Boomtown Rats' "I Don't Like Mondays" on Monday mornings in the eighties. The song composed by Bob Geldof reached the top of the British charts in July 1979. The idea for the song came to Geldof after he heard about the terrible shooting on Monday, January 29, 1979, in San Diego, California. A sixteen-year-old teenager, Brenda Ann Spencer, opened fire on a group of kids playing in the schoolyard of the Cleveland Elementary School across the street from her house. Two were killed, nine others injured. Feeling no remorse at all for what she'd done, Brenda Ann Spencer justified her actions by saying she simply didn't like Mondays and wanted to put a little bit of spice in her boring day. American rock stations played "I Don't Like Mondays" on Monday mornings in the eighties. Except in San Diego, out of respect for the families of the victims.

April 20, 1999, Columbine. Thirteen dead. Two teenagers armed to the teeth wreak havoc in a Colorado school. They kill themselves after carrying out their carnage.

July 29, 1999. A man kills nine innocent people in two Atlanta, Georgia, day-trading outfits after having reportedly murdered his wife and two children. He would kill himself a few hours later.

October 2002. John Allen Muhammad fires on people

filling up their gas tanks in the American capital's service stations during twenty-three days of pure paranoia.

October 2, 2006, Nickel Mines, Pennsylvania. A father living an otherwise peaceful existence barricades himself in an Amish school. He lines up five girls and a teenager in front of the blackboard in a classroom, ties their feet before executing them in cold blood by shooting them in the head. After the massacre, he kills himself.

April 16, 2007. On Virginia Tech's campus, a student commits the most murderous mass shooting in US history up to that point. Thirty-two people die from gunshot wounds before the murderer kills himself.

October 16, 2008. A shooting on the lawn in front of Henry Ford Elementary School in Detroit kills one and injures three. An unidentified man steps out of his car, fires on the children, returns to his car, and disappears.

April 2, 2012, Oakland. A man kills seven in a college in Northern California.

July 20, 2012, Aurora. James Holmes opens fire in a movie theatre outside Denver, Colorado, during the projection of Christopher Nolan's *Batman Begins*. He kills twelve and injures fifty-eight others.

I Am Charlie Decker

Due to the frequency of these tragedies, new expressions have come into existence: "school shooter," "school massacre," "school shooting," "code black," "lockdown." How do you come to the decision to start murdering six- or seven-year-olds in an elementary school? Researchers with the American secret service can't seem to establish a clear profile for these types of killers. They aren't necessarily committing a thoughtless act when they open fire on a classroom full of students: they plan their acts meticulously, buy weapons, confide in others about their plans. Contrary to what we believe, the killers don't inevitably come from broken single-parent homes; some had the perfect family life. And if there are loners among them or bullied kids, most don't fit neatly into those categories.

* * *

On Friday, January 25, 2013, Stephen King published a text demanding stricter gun control legislation in his country. The online essay, that sold for ninety-nine cents, is called *Guns*. He calls for an outright ban on assault weapons and large capacity magazines. There is another old debate, one we don't have a clear answer for: does fiction simply mirror an increasingly violent reality, or does it stoke the flames by inspiring increasingly barbaric acts?

Stephen King has always believed that a person doesn't suddenly become murderous because he's read a book or watched a film or listened to an album. According to King, the problem is found in the fact that it's far too easy to obtain firearms in the United States. However, in 1999, King took one of his novels out of circulation: *Rage*, published in 1977, under the pseudonym Richard Bachman. In the book, a high school student, Charlie Decker, takes his class hostage after having killed his math teacher.

April 26, 1988, Jeffrey Lyne Cox turns his semi-automatic rifle on his classmates at San Gabriel High School in California. He's brought down before going through with his act. Cox read *Rage* many times. Psychologically unstable, Cox liked to believe he was Charlie Decker.

September 18, 1989. Dustin L. Pierce takes a class hostage in a Kentucky high school. His arsenal mortifies the sequestered students: a hunting rifle and two pistols. Nine hours later, he turns himself into the cops. A copy of *Rage* was found in his room.

February 2, 1996, Moses Lake, Washington State. Barry Loukaitis murders two students and a math teacher. A few days earlier, Loukaitis was bullied. Reading *Rage*, according to the murderer during his trial, was a major turning point in his life. Barry Loukaitis was only fourteen.

December 1, 1997. Michael Carneal, also aged fourteen, shoots at a prayer group in his Kentucky high school at point-blank range. Eight shots are fired: three people, all young girls, are killed. Five others are injured. A copy of *Rage* is found in the murderer's locker.

Following the Columbine massacre on April 20, 1999, Stephen King asked for his novel to be taken out of print.

King, a typical American, paradoxically keeps three guns at home, with a "clear conscience." Those are his words.

Chaos

Everything passes. Pain passes, even joy and euphoria pass. People like to remind you of that with their comforting words. They play the wise men who've seen it all before. Oh, how they take pleasure in saying that everything will be all right, that time heals, that time mends, scars fade. Life continues, they drone, filled with good intentions. They haven't understood a thing.

In moments of great tragedy, we can judge the sheer magnitude of the vanity, the emptiness, the absurdity of our existences. And the disappearance of someone close to you, a mother, a child, is the most painful of these tragedies. The agonizing reality of it doesn't fade by talking about it, or letting time go about its usual way.

Sophocles spoke a sad truth: "For when men lose the joys that sweeten life, I cannot count this living, rather deem as of a breathing corpse." Everything can disappear in an instant: you must never take anything for granted. The ground can fall away beneath you at any moment. And then powerless, you're forced to witness your universe derailing. Nothing else matters when it happens, nothing at all.

In ancient Greek, *khaos* refers to a chasm, a void. We can see *khaos* as an indistinct and empty state, the planet before God's creation, before His intervention. A sort of confused state of matter that has not yet been organized and structured into what we would call the *cosmos*.

When a great tragedy occurs in a human being's life, we sometimes see the opposite of organization: from the *cosmos,* the blessed interlude where every river runs down from its source, a sort of predictable, reassuring structure, we move back into *khaos.* Our landmarks become foreign, we become aware that everything the comfortable construction of our lives stood on can come tumbling down like a house of cards. We become aware of the precariousness of the edifice of our existence.

And then the charitable souls arrive, sad donkeys come to bray, to attempt without conviction to maintain us in a cosmological orbit of sorts, a place where everything is full of meaning, is meaningful. They deliver their bland, hackneyed phrases in a simultaneous attempt to consolidate their idyllic understanding of life and rebuild yours. They drone on about how everything happens for a reason, like others might say that what doesn't kill you makes you stronger.

My mother never had any theoretical notions of philosophy or knowledge of classical thinkers. She wasn't very educated, she was a woman of intuition, of common sense. She wasn't the sort to lean on popular psycho-babble, a sort of *easy listening* for souls seeking landmarks. That sort of bullshit never consoled her, nor did the moralizing Scriptures that were the staple of her Catholic upbringing.

While those close to her spent most of their time looking for meaning behind their pain—and even often convinced themselves they'd found the reason behind it all—my mother would have gladly consented to sinking like a stone into a muddy lake had she not been secured by a cocktail of powerful antidepressants and anxiolytics. A socially acceptable junky, thanks to great advances in pharmacology. Without her drugs, she would have drifted out of orbit and into the void. Twice, she lost her sense of direction. The second time cast her into the abyss of depression for good. No, nothing has meaning. An infinite black hole.

* * *

Carmen handed me the keys to apartment 21, where my mother had lived for the last two years of her life. I bombarded mom's neighbour with questions. I wanted to understand, even if I intuitively knew all the details. She formulated her story in incoherent morsels.

On the afternoon of Monday, February 11, my mother confided in her neighbour that she was going to end her life. She simply couldn't hang on anymore. She said that it was worse than in '84. I knew the reference too well. My mother had expressed this through a veil of sobs. She seemed delirious. Among her disjointed jumble, she mentioned the hammer a few times ("The hammer! The hammer!" was Carmen's theatrical imitation of her panicked friend), a cornfield behind the house, and Christiane, her twin sister who vanished.

After having calmed down a little, my mother ended up asking Carmen to leave her alone, a little before five. She then asked Carmen to come to her apartment with her spare key in the early evening of the next day, Tuesday. Around seven, not before. She left her my phone number as well, which Carmen would dial to give me the news of the discovery of my mother's cold, inanimate body.

Worse than in '84, indeed. Black Tuesday.

Chronicle of a Death Foretold

Perhaps I played an involuntary role in the precipitation of those tragic events. I will never know for sure, and I need to make efforts of self-persuasion to distract myself from the idea that could easily eat me alive.

On the afternoon on Monday, February 11, 2013, I called my mother. I told her I had some time off and didn't have any plans for the next day, Tuesday. I offered to run a few errands for her, and even, why not, cook a few meals she could freeze for another day. And while I was at it, I could clean the bathroom and wash the floors. She said she was with her neighbor Carmen, and asked me to call back in the evening so we could arrange the details.

Towards seven, I called her again, but her attitude had changed completely. She was closed off, more distant than earlier in the afternoon. She sounded rather out of it, depressed; nothing new. I knew more than anyone else that mom had her bad days. She insisted I shouldn't come. She wanted to be alone. Anyway, an orderly from the community health centre would come over on the weekend to clean the place up. As for errands, Carmen would take care of them. It wasn't worth it for me to drive all the way to Joliette.

I was irritated by her stubbornness. I simply didn't have as much patience as I used to when it came to the tantrums of this bitter old woman. I insisted, and she refused again, asking me to respect her decision. And that was final.

Increasingly impatient, I explained that since I wouldn't have the opportunity to visit over the next few days, it would be great to kill two birds with one stone. She refused again, reminding me that she was perfectly capable of taking care of herself. "Why don't you live your life without worrying about me, okay?" she said dryly.

I saw red. Knowing it was impossible to get her not to be as stubborn as a mule, I decided to end the debate: "Fine. If that's how you want it... You can call me whenever you decide you want to see me. You know where to reach me." Since the moment I hung up the phone that day, I feel I've been drowning in the glacial silence of that failed conversation.

* * *

Fade to black.

Tuesday.

The next day, following the plan to have breakfast with a cousin in Joliette before going to my mother's place, I drove towards the city where the ingrate I had on the phone the previous day lived. What sort of mother refuses to see her son? And what could I do? I drove towards La Cafèt', a restaurant in downtown Joliette, for a bite with my cousin, Rose.

To obey my mother's capricious desires, I decided I simply wouldn't stop by and visit her. I was motivated by one part pettiness, certainly, a few parts pride, but mostly sulky resentment. An ambulance siren shook me out of my acrimonious thoughts and I pulled over to the right to let the emergency vehicle through.

I reached the restaurant and met up with a hale, smiling

Rose. We spent part of our hour together carping about our respective mothers, since both had become cantankerous to the point of being unbearable. The release changed nothing about our family relationship, but at least it made me realize I wasn't the only one with a frustrating mother.

After breakfast, I made my way to the used bookstore to drop off a box of old books in exchange for a few bucks immediately spent at the record store on the other side of the street. The same record store where I had first discovered, thirty years prior, my favourite bands. I even found unsold discs from another time: Joy Division, The Cure (*Faith* and *Pornography*), The Sex Pistols, The Boomtown Rats, Marvin Gaye....

A wave of nostalgia came over me in that place where I used to love whiling away the days with my pals when I was fifteen or sixteen. Memories, not all good ones, of those days when, completely unprepared, I was forced to become the psychological support for a mother as brittle as glass.

Just as I was about to get back on the road, I decided to swallow my pride and go visit Mom. I'd help her, the old ingrate, even against her will.

I reached her apartment building, a home for autonomous elderly people with limited means. I hesitated before going upstairs to knock on her door. Would she see it as provocation, or disobedience? She could be so vindictive. Or maybe a sign of weakness, as if I was just dying of guilt after having hung up on her the night before. No matter, who could blame me at my age for disobeying a stubborn old woman?

Just as I was about to walk into the building, two residents chatting away on the doorstep looked at me sideways. They asked me whether I was there to visit Mrs. Forest. My answer was met with a look of ill omen, and I could tell the two were wondering how to break some terrible news, evaluating which one of them would be the most delicate in pronouncing the sentence.

After a brief but uncomfortable moment in which I felt tension climbing my spine, one of the residents informed me that my mother had been taken to the hospital by an ambulance, a little more than an hour earlier. When she was carried past them on the stretcher, my mother was cold, at least according to what they heard one of the paramedics say. The two women continued speaking, their voices mingling in my head with the noise of a torrent rushing through a narrow riverbed.

I absorbed the news stoically. I felt like I was being emptied from the inside out.

Why don't you live your life without worrying about me, okay?

That winter morning, a chasm opened up under my feet. An endless drop, vertiginous, as if I was falling in every direction at once. At the wheel of my car as I drove towards the hospital, I was surprisingly calm. As soon as I noticed my stillness, I rebuked myself for it. I felt like I was foundering beneath dark waters. That's the right word: foundering. As if I was disintegrating, crumbling, becoming jetsam.

Fade to Black

Of the seven dwarves in *Snow White*, only Dopey's image (the Disney version of it) appears on the door to Danny's room in the Boulder apartment. You can see him on the wall, on the left side of the screen, a clear image of the hairless, mute dwarf. It's a traveling shot, guiding the viewer towards Danny's first experience with the *shining*. He's alone with his double (Tony), facing the bathroom mirror which reflects terrifying, bloody scenes: two elevator shafts, torrents of blood pouring out of them, litres and litres of Kubrick-red liquid, and two young blond girls dressed in sky-blue dresses.

Dopey is renowned for his cowardice, though he's able to come to Snow White's defense in times of need...

A few minutes later, when we see Danny's door for the second time, Dopey's image has disappeared from its original location. A simple continuity mistake? Perhaps, even for the perfectionist Kubrick. However, it might just be that in the eyes of the filmmaker, after his first encounter with the *shining*, Danny Torrance is no longer akin to the silly, fun-loving Dopey.

* * *

I notice an image over Danny's bed, in his room in the Overlook. Two bears that recall the scene where Danny is being examined by the doctor in his room in Boulder, resting on a pillow in the shape of a brown bear. He has just emerged from the deep, from a strange sort of blackout. His hands are joined in front of him, seemingly protecting his genitalia. The doctor asks him whether his alter ego, Tony, asks him to do things sometimes. Danny cuts the conversations short, saying he prefers not to speak of Tony.

* * *

I was a teenager when a well-informed classmate told me the main lines of the tragedy of 1942. It was as if I had just received a hammer blow to the back of the head. A first loss of innocence...

Back home that afternoon, I went to my mother, bursting with questions, oblivious to her friend Solange with her in the kitchen helping her empty the Dominion shopping bags. I remember too well she observed me for a few seconds, as long as eternity, before saying anything.

We lived in Saint-Alexis at the time, a small village where the tragedies of the past live long before sinking beneath the waters of forgetfulness. That day, I discovered the tragedy of my maternal grandparent. I didn't react, it was as if the story was about strangers. What could I have said? I was barely a teenager, sorry about events I couldn't change.

It would take time before I could see the impact this tragic past might have had on my fragile mother's life. From then on, I considered her differently. As if I had just found an answer to a mysterious enigma. From that day on, I became obsessed with uncovering hidden truths.

Corn Flakes and André Gide

"In a work of art I rather like to find transposed, on the scale of characters, the very subject of that work [...] [as] the device of heraldry that consists in setting in the escutcheon a smaller one *'en abyme,'* at the heart-point."

Directed in 1971 by Robert Mulligan, *Summer of '42* is known as being Stanley Kubrick's favourite movie. It's the story of fifteen-year-old Hermie (Gary Grimes) falling under the spell of Dorothy (Jennifer O'Neill), married and twice his age.

A scene out of *The Shining* shows Wendy and Danny Torrance in the living room of the hotel watching the Mulligan-directed movie. The scene out of *Summer* Kubrick shows us is the one where Hermie helps Dorothy carry her groceries into her house. *Summer of '42*'s plot is in no way linked to Kubrick's own movie. Instead, we should consider the title, the historical connotation of the date in question, the summer of 1942, the middle of an apocalypse.

Over the course of that summer, the German army won an almost uninterrupted string of victories. Europe, crushed under its boot heel, trembles. In September 1942, in Poland, the extermination of the Warsaw ghetto begins. Following the godforsaken *Selektion*, only thirty-five thousand Jews are left in this antechamber of the death camps. Ten times fewer people than were originally in the ghetto.

This massacre and the ones that succeeded it came to take on barely conceivable proportions. The deafening staccato of Adler typewriters tear through the terrorized silence of Eastern Europe's grey streets.

* * *

When I was my daughter's age—Aurore is her name—the box of Corn Flakes had a picture of a child eating his cereal in front of a box of Corn Flakes on which there must have been a child eating his cereal in front of a box of Corn Flakes on which there must have been...and so on. The child I was, eating his Corn Flakes, felt sucked in by the image on the box. An enchanting invitation, made doubly attractive by an extra spoonful of sugar.

* * *

The scene in which the Torrance family drives towards the Overlook Hotel has a striking *mise en abyme*—non-narrational self-reflexivity as scholarly parlance goes, though that phrase never feels as powerful as its French counterpart, literally meaning *placed into the abyss*. There is a sort of micro/macro reflection. As such, the seemingly anodyne discussion the trio has about a group of pioneers stuck in the Colorado Rockies and forced to resort to cannibalism foreshadows *The Shining*'s murderous insanity.

* * *

I like the idea of a box of cereal as heraldry. Who knows whether, when I was seven, a child eating his Corn Flakes watched me as I let myself be absorbed by the image of a child on a box of Corn Flakes. Who knows whether—a little like that image of Jack Torrance on the photo dated July 4, 1921, at the end of the movie—I might not then find myself in some parallel universe, or in an anodyne *mise en abyme* on a box of Corn Flakes. *Ad infinitum*.

Prodigies

Some have perfect pitch: without training or musical references, without even being able to read an "F" on a stave, these prodigies can intuitively reproduce, in their integrality, a melody they heard once.

Others can play ten games of chess at once without even looking at the boards. They can memorize the position of the thirty-two pieces on the sixty-four squares of the board. They can anticipate in a phenomenal manner what might happen next, and a smaller number can checkmate their opponents without ever looking at the action. It won't surprise you to learn that Stanley Kubrick was known to play chess. Several photographs show him on one film set or another, concentrated on a chessboard during a pause between scenes, playing the game where the important pieces have doubles of the same color (two bishops, two rooks, two knights) and where each piece finds its counterpart in the other camp (the king, the queen, the pawns). He was likely seduced by the balance, the constructed duality of the board.

Other people can, simply by glancing at an article in the newspaper, tell you without fail how many occurrences of a certain letter you'll find in the copy. These people are gifted, bestowed by nature with a little something more.

Duello Finale

"They did their own thing, like everybody else. A young couple, they never bothered anyone. They led a totally normal life. You never saw them angry or anything. I didn't hear a thing, or I would have called 9-1-1. We can be thankful the kids weren't home that weekend. There are toys just lying in their yard. Isn't that strange?" (*Abitibi Express*, October 8, 2011)

"Their father picked them up around 5:30 in the afternoon, after work on Friday. Everything seemed normal. Little William left holding his dad's hand, with the gift he made for Mother's Day in a little pink bag he decorated." (*La Nouvelle Union*, May 10, 2011)

"Around 10:00 in the morning, we received a call to go check up on an address: 3531, Rue Beaudry, in Joliette. The officers found the body of a woman. Around the same time, our officers were responding to an emergency call related to a possible suicide in Saint-Charles-Borromée." (*L'action*, February 5, 2008)

"We can't believe it. They moved in not too long ago. I just can't believe it. I've got a lot of family in the area, you know, and I got really worried when I heard about it on television." (*Le Journal de Montréal*, November 22, 2004)

"The Quebec Provincial Police confirmed that the two children sometimes stayed at the residence of the reconstituted family, but that they were not present at the time of the tragedy. According to information we received, the youngest of the children was staying with a friend of the family, while the other was with his biological mother." (*Hebdo Rive-Nord*, May 13, 2013)

"My living room window gives onto their backyard. They were a couple with kids about the same age as ours. They got here last fall. We were happy to have neighbours with young children. Our children could have become friends. I never heard any sort of fighting coming from their house. Nothing could lead us to believe it would end like this. We're a small village here, you know, and everyone knows everyone else. I just don't know what to think anymore." (*Le Reflet du lac*, May 22, 2002)

"Mrs. Aurore Forest (nee Pauzé), twenty-four years of age, was found dead in her home last Monday, September 7, on Main Street in Saint-Alexis. Not long after, the body of her husband Dr. Jacques Forest, 31, was discovered by a neighbour. Evidence points to Dr. Forest having murdered his wife before taking his own life in the minutes that followed his odious act. The Quebec Provincial Police is investigating the case as a murder-suicide." (*L'Étoile du Nord*, September 9, 1942)

* * *

Some people just attract tragedy like flies to shit. As best she could, my mother, Danielle Forest, survived the torment of a childhood marked by an angry drunk of a father. The man they called in the village of Saint-Alexis "the good doctor Forest" wasn't without blame, though the community said it could have never anticipated the terrible acts of Sunday, September 6, 1942. They all believed he led an exemplary life.

In old photographs, we see a wife, always smiling. Two happy kids with curly blond hair. A respected profession. A social status the envy of the community. Alderman on the council and churchwarden for the parish. People took their hats off to greet him when, on Sunday morning, they passed him on Main Street. That day, all of Montcalm County, maybe even the greater Lanaudière region, suffered a blow. The good Dr. Jacques Forest caused shock and horror in his community when he staved in his wife's skull with a hammer as she was sitting at her kitchen table, reading in silence, in their house on Main Street, in Saint-Alexis.

Dead End

Mazes, by their nature, are the ultimate *dead ends*. Isn't that right, *mister* Torrance?

* * *

September 1942. When they were five, twin sisters Danielle and Christiane Forest went missing for three days. They were found only a few hundred metres away from their now condemned house, bent and contorted, in an endless cornfield where they had found refuge for three days and three nights.

* * *

On a sunny Sunday afternoon towards the end of the summer, about an hour after getting home from mass, Christiane Forest fell off the swing set-up on the oak tree near the family home, after being pushed a bit too hard by her twin sister, Danielle. She cut open her knee as she fell. Red stained her white socks. She always did have a violent aversion for blood. She immediately rushed towards the family home to get her nasty cut tended to. Just as they were about to open the screen door, the girls were struck stock-still. A horror scene unfolding, one which would traumatize them both for the rest of their lives: their father, covered in blood, smashing their mother's head over and over again with a hammer. Another blow, and another still, and a last one, again. Jacques Forest's sky-blue shirt stained with the blood of his wife, her head resting against the kitchen table. Inert. A rag doll. Playing together outside a minute before, Danielle and Christiane hadn't heard a single shout. Likely because Aurore Pauzé was knocked on her head from behind without ever anticipating the first blow.

On the other side of the screen door opening onto the kitchen, the two girls, in a state of shock, stood unmoving, hand in hand. Not a sound, except for Jacques Forest's ragged breathing. Red liquid pooling on the table, dripping to the floor. The sheer quantity of it, unbearable.

They ran. The noise of their shoes on the wooden deck alerted the father, who immediately understood his daughters had witnessed the execution. He burst out of the house, shouting Danielle's name, then Christiane's. In tears, he howled, ordering his children to come home. A mad dog barking. He ran a few dozen metres, chasing the girls, but quickly enough realized he wouldn't catch them. He gave up, fell, prostrated. Jacques Forest wailed the name of his daughters again, in vain. In the distance, a dog howled.

The two sisters managed to escape their mother's executioner by having the good fortune and reflexes to run behind the house and towards the immense cornfield owned by the Landry family, their closest neighbours. Over the past month, they'd been playing hide-and-seek in the field with their friends. As the girls hid in silence, they could hear him crying, shouting, a storm unbound. "Danielle! Christiane!" Then, nothing. Hidden, safe in the opaque maze of corn stalks twice as high as they were, the Forest sisters, it seems, barely made it out alive.

When night fell, Danielle and Christiane felt the cold in their bones. At the end of the summer, nights are cool, especially when you spend them outside in your Sunday best. They thought they might freeze to death in the cornfield. They got hungry during those long days hidden there. Even if their mother had just been killed in front of their eyes, hunger ate at them. They would end up losing consciousness from exhaustion, but not the first night, terrorized at the idea of being found by their father gone mad. A man they didn't recognize anymore. If he murdered their mother, there was a risk he would do the same to them. It was impossible to give in to sleep. Christiane choked back her sobs, they came out as mere squeaks. Tears rolling down her cheeks, she murmured, over and over again: "Mom, mom." Danielle stayed stoic, seemingly paralyzed. Nervous shock. Not a tear, not a noise, unable to speak. Danielle cradled her sister in her arms. Sitting on the ground in the middle of the cornstalks, they spent three days and three nights waiting. Listening. Without daring to come out. Their survival instinct.

Finally, they heard voices. Their names shouted out by men and women approaching their hiding place. Uncertain, they didn't dare make a peep, didn't dare move, until they heard Ms. Landry's voice. As soon as they recognized their neighbour, they got up, advanced in the direction of the voice through the tall cornstalks. The girls were immediately surrounded by dozens of villagers who'd been participating in the search. Two men took the weakened girls in their arms and rushed them to the Landry home. The sisters' grandparents, on the Pauzé side, were sitting on the deck in front of the house, their faces drawn, visibly exhausted. After having recognized their granddaughters, realizing they were safe and sound, they rushed forward to kiss them, to tell them, over and over again, that everything would be okay.

* * *

Two days before they were found, on Monday morning, Jacques Forest was discovered by a neighbour. He was hanging in his shed, the one next to the house. The man had come to wish him a nice day and ask for his advice about his leg that had been strangely numb for a few days. The tragedy likely occurred the day before, on September 6, 1942.

Less than a week after the girls' universe exploded along with their mother's skull, Danielle and Christiane were taken in by their mother's parents. They too were trying to deal with unbearable pain. The Pauzé grandparents gathered them in with as much love and tenderness as they could muster. According to family lore, my mother, especially my mother, was a difficult child.

Labyrinths

"**T**his whole place is such an enormous maze, I feel I'll have to leave a trail of breadcrumbs every time I come in," Mrs. Torrance jokingly tells Dick Hallorann the day the hotel closes for the winter. Hadn't Wendy learned that the breadcrumbs never helped Hansel and Gretel?

* * *

A scholarly journal about myth and criticism, *Amaltea*, tells us about the origin and symbolism of mazes and labyrinths. The first one that comes to mind in mythology, the Labyrinth of Crete, was built by an architect, Daedalus, under orders of King Minos, to imprison the Minotaur. More commonly, we refer to labyrinths and mazes as places made of a considerable number of rooms and galleries whose disposition makes any hope of escape difficult. Most who adventure inside never come out.

Etymologically, the word labyrinth comes from the Greek *labyrinthos*, "the house of labrys." And what does *labrys* mean? "Double-edged axe," as luck would have it. We speak here of an axe that wasn't only used for defense, but also reflects the useful work of the plough, whose defining characteristic is a well-sharpened ploughshare. Etymologically, the word labyrinth means the double-edged house. Originally, the double-edged axe was the emblem of the Kings of Minoan. Metonymy brings us the house of the man with the double-edged axe, meaning the king. The labyrinth is thus simply the house of Minos.

But, more fundamentally, the labyrinth is a place of entrails, the place for a rite of passage in which one dies and is reborn, the psychological process necessary if one aspires to significant transformation. We can consider this mess of corridors and tunnels like a mortal trap for those who dare enter it. Until, of course, Theseus' famous and fortunate crossing. He who, after having brought the Minotaur low, found his way back thanks to Ariadne's famous thread, which he had uncoiled behind him to guide his way.

* * *

My daughter, Aurore, is as good at following the thread of a labyrinth on paper as you might read MURDER in the inscription REꓷЯUM if you placed it in front of a mirror. While I sometimes fail to find the exit on intermediate labyrinths, she can successfully navigate even the most complex ones as if it were child's play. Aurore barely needs more than twenty seconds to concentrate on the image, giving herself an overall view of her sinuous path. Once she's assimilated the image, she then easily traces an uninterrupted line from the entrance to the exit, avoiding all impasses and frustrating dead ends. It's funny to consider that I thought of naming her Ariadne before she was born, before settling on Aurore.

Delbert Grady

Can we still speak, seventy years later, of collateral victims of a foul murder? Is it possible for me to still be hearing the echoes of the hammer blows dealt to my grandmother when my own mother was only five?

After having seen *The Shining* an uncountable number of times, I can claim that this movie is beyond simple calculations. *Forever, and ever, and ever*. Nor does time have any sway over the eternal boarders of the Overlook Hotel. Clearly, there's something unconscious at play here, in the way *The Shining* imposed itself as the beacon that guides my way along the saturnine labyrinth of my macabre lineage. In fact, could it be that my unhealthy obsession with Kubrick's extraordinary work ignites in me a dark passion for horror? Am I intrinsically attracted to it like a moth to a flame?

The Shining might be my personal Overlook, in which I'm condemned to wander *forever, and ever, and ever*. That would make my grandparent Jacques Forest my own personal Delbert Grady. Smashing my grandmother's skull with his bloody hammer, it's as if he'd nailed a rusty nail forged in the '40s into his two daughters and his grandson born a quarter century later. The Dark Ages, as they say.

At the Far End of the Paths of Glory

I n 1957, Stanley Kubrick directed *Paths of Glory*, with Kirk Douglas playing the lead role. In this movie set during the First World War, we find two themes dear to Kubrick: duality and the portrait of a world in ruin.

During the filming, he met the German actor Christiane Harlan, whom he would marry in 1958; her brother, Jan Harlan, would later be *The Shining*'s producer. *Paths of Glory* should be seen if only for the trench scenes which prefigure Jack Torrance's hunt in the cedar maze.

Christiane Harlan Kubrick is the niece of Veit Harlan, a German film director. He produced propaganda films under the Third Reich, including *Kolberg*, in 1945, under Goebbels' orders. The movie's purpose was to strengthen the morale of the *Wehrmacht* troops and that of the German people. Accused of crimes against humanity in 1948, Veit Harlan would be acquitted one year later.

Christiane Harlan Kubrick would be Stanley Kubrick's partner for forty-two years, until March 7, 1999, when death intervened. Forty-two years together, no more, no less.

Dark Cult

December 29, 1945, the notorious sociopath Ed Gein is completely destroyed by his mother's death, she who exercised a considerable ascendency over him, even if he was thirty-nine years old. Poorly equipped to handle the outside world on his own, he isolated himself, rejected the truth of his mother's death, trying to bring her back to life by chanting incantations in front of her grave.

It helps to know that, throughout his childhood, Ed Gein was forced to dress like a girl by his mother. As an adult, he continued to do so. During the night, in the cemetery, he would play the resurrectionist by digging up the cadavers of women with a shovel. He cut the skin from the exhumed bodies and sowed himself a human dress. Ed Gein, then, literally dressed as a woman.

* * *

Scabrous events are nothing new. They used to sell copies, now they accumulate *likes* on social media. The abominable scumbag that is a killer becomes a money-maker once we turn him into a pop culture icon. We all know Jack the Ripper, but who could name off the top of their head a single one of his victims? The killer from Whitechapel might have been the first to profit from the publicity freely given by journalists covering his sordid acts. *Extra! Extra! Jack the Ripper strikes again!* Since 1888 a dark cult has developed around heinous murders, analogous and parallel to our devotion to celebrities. The tabloids as we know them feed and are fed by these killers.

* * *

It's worth asking if bloodthirsty and cruel killers are a product of our society gone mad. Have murderers always been part of our constellation? Is there a constant of violence in the human condition? Then we shouldn't pretend: we should just give up. Abandon all hope. Might just be the pessimist's answer to the problem.

Most horror stories teach us one thing: it's not the psychopath or the serial killer you need to fear most among all the foul things in our unstable society; no, you should fear your neighbours, the man or the woman sitting on the stool next to you in the bar, the failed writer, the village's good doctor. Yourself. We are the big bad wolves of the stories we were told as children.

By revealing the vile impulses of the father, the head of the family, *The Shining* goes beyond the simple and enjoyable spooky story. The darkness of humanity leads us to understand something: man is the most shameful of all creatures who ever walked or crawled on this earth. The link between fairytales (*Thumbelina*, *Snow White*, *Bluebeard*, *The Three Little Pigs*, *Hansel and Gretel*) and the movie *The Shining*—stuffed with references to these stories—forces us to stare at the reflection of our deepest fears—the inner darkness of man. This is the essential character of our secular oral traditions. And thus the timeless quality of Kubrick's movie.

The Shining, like other works in the same genre, is a barely modified retelling of traditional stories. Bluebeard, the big bad wolf, the ogre, the cruel stepmother, the witch are all timeless characters—archetypes—that we simply decided to name differently—psychopath, sociopath, mass murderer, psycho killer, school shooter, pedophile. Even though the new stories are the same as the old ones, told over and over, they warn the reader, the viewer, the listener against Evil.

In his fascinating thriller *Brother Grimm*, the Scotsman Craig Russell makes an eloquent demonstration: reality inspires fiction which inspires reality...Gilles de Rais, Conomor the Cursed, and so many others inspired the creation of the mythical character Bluebeard. From his isolated farm in Plainfield, Wisconsin, didn't Ed Gein create Norman Bates (*Psycho*) and Buffalo Bill (*The Silence of the Lambs*)? Chairs and stools made of human bones and a suit made of the skin of exhumed corpses were discovered in Ed Gein's house. And yet, once again, these scabrous and quite real details, worthy of the most terrifying horror films, are simply pulled out of the old Russian tales of Baba Yaga, and her cabin on chicken legs with its bone furniture. Following that line of thought, what real story inspired the creation of Baba Yaga, what danger was the story warning us against?

And what if Stanley Kubrick was trying to tell us that we are, even in violence and cruelty, only variations on the same theme? What if his *Shining* helped demonstrate that we repeat our mistakes over and over again? There is no exit, we are condemned to repeat the same calamities generation after generation, century after century.

"When I came up here for my interview, it was as though

I had been here before. We . . . we all have moments of déjà vu, but this was ridiculous. It was almost as though I knew what was going to be around every corner." (Jack Torrance speaking to Wendy, a month after reaching the Overlook.)

Everything repeats itself in an eternal cycle. Recurrence is almost necessary. Delbert Grady, Charles Grady, Jack Torrance, and this impossible final image where we recognize Jack's face in the picture taken during the Independence Day ball, on July 4, 1921. All the same. No matter the time, the era, there will always be someone to repeat the same atrocities. Jacques Forest killed my grandmother with frightful blows of his hammer, and yet he was only aping the same crimes that have occurred since time immemorial, an unconscious extension of ancestral atavism.

Perhaps all the attention given to *The Shining* and Jack Torrance's murderous project is justified by the same logic. Perhaps we're all trapped in the labyrinthine corridors of the Overlook, searching for an answer to the existential questions gnawing at us. Perhaps we think we'll find the answers just around the corner of a corridor that we have a vague but persistent impression of having walked through at some point, some time before.

REDЯUM on the Wall

The Bible tells us that King Belshazzar, son of Neb-uchadnezzar, saw a mysterious hand appear, which proceeded to write his own death warrant on the wall of his palace in Babylon.

We find this anecdote prophesying the fall of Belshazzar in the Book of Daniel.

"In the same hour came forth fingers of a man's hand, and wrote over against the candlestick upon the plaster of the wall of the king's palace: and the king saw the part of the hand that wrote. Then the king's countenance was changed, and his thoughts troubled him, so that the joints of his loins were loosed, and his knees smote one against another." (Daniel 5: 5-6)

* * *

Danny seems to be in a trance, standing next to his mother, kitchen knife in his left hand. In his right hand he holds his mother's lipstick. On the door to her room, he writes the letters R-E-D-Я-U-M. In the mirror, REDЯUM seen reversed gives us MURDER. Over and over again, Danny repeats tonelessly: "Redrum!" Exactly forty-two times.

* * *

My seven-year-old daughter doesn't know that the animated movie she's watching borrowed a number of ideas and scenes from *The Shining*. She doesn't recognize the pattern on the carpet in the house of the psychopathic Sid in *Toy Story*. She doesn't know the movie's director, Jon Lasseter, is referencing the Overlook Hotel's own maze-like carpets. Similarly, Aurore is still too young to understand why the mutant toy, as he pulls himself out of the sandbox to begin ambling towards young Sid, speaks in a disembodied voice: REDRUM. And how old will she be the day I'll dare hand her the Kubrick-red book of her macabre lineage?

REDRUM!
REDRUM! REDRUM! REDRUM!
REDRUM! REDRUM! REDRUM!
REDRUM! REDRUM! REDRUM! REDRUM!
REDRUM! REDRUM! REDRUM!
REDRUM! REDRUM! REDRUM!
REDRUM!
REDRUM! REDRUM! REDRUM!
REDRUM! REDRUM! REDRUM!
REDRUM! REDRUM! REDRUM!
REDRUM! REDRUM!
REDRUM! REDRUM! REDRUM! REDRUM!
REDRUM! REDRUM! REDRUM! REDRUM!
REDRUM! REDRUM! REDRUM! REDRUM!
REDRUM!

Meep Meep

The sheer number of children exposed to violence committed by one parent on another is, to say the least, troubling. Broken dishes, doors slammed, shouts, cries, insults, a hand tightening around an arm, a throat, a shove, a slap, a punch, a threat, an ultimatum; the oppressive performance of domestic life. According to the best research, these children will be more likely to ape, as adults, the same cycle of violence, shameful slaves to the pattern of received abuse.

Twice, during *The Shining*, Danny Torrance watches cartoons on television. Both times, it's the *Road Runner*. A character created by Chuck Jones in 1949, the Road Runner contributed to *Looney Tunes'* extraordinary success, about just as much as Bugs Bunny himself—*What's up, Doc?* In the first scene, set in the Torrance apartment in Boulder, we recognize the show thanks to the characteristic soundtrack interspersed by a familiar *meep meep!* or two, as the long-legged roadrunner escapes the traps set by the famished coyote.

Towards the end of Kubrick's movie, we even get the cartoon's theme: *"Road Runner, the coyote's after you, Road Runner, if he catches you you're through."* At this point Danny, disturbed by his visions, is kept locked away from his father gone mad. So the child watches television, almost hypnotized, dressed in his red pajamas. Just like my daughter, Aurore, seven and a half, the bearded director of *The Shining* knew his Saturday morning classics.

Child Star

I know what became of Danny Lloyd. I also know Michael Cera stars in popular comedies. I know what became of Nathalie Simard. I know who the second victim of the lecherous impresario was. I know Marie-Josée Taillefer appears on Radio-Canada. I know Natalie Portman is quite beautiful. I may never know what happened to Madeleine McCann. I know Marie-Soleil Tougas didn't get a chance to age. I have no idea what terrible traumatic disorders the children who survived the Sandy Hook killing will have. I've been thinking about it a lot, recently. What happened to Virginie Larivière? I know Daniel Lloyd teaches science in a college in Missouri. I don't know if Daniel Lloyd was watching CNN on December 14, 2012. I don't know if he hid his face with his hands when the planet learned about a tiny city in Connecticut.

"Tony, I'm scared."

"Remember what Mr. Hallorann said. It's just like pictures in a book, Danny. It isn't real."

You wish. But no, Danny, it's real. The ugliest fucking reality that reality has to offer, this time. The movie's over. Cut!

I know Danny Lloyd, the biology professor, has children. I know that when his children saw their father in Stanley Kubrick's movie, they made fun of his haircut. I wonder if, to make them laugh, Daddy Danny sometimes takes Tony's rasping voice, moving his right index finger. What? Can't we laugh a little? Just to make it easier to bear?

Tennis

"Mr. Hallorann, what is in Room 237?"

It's a tennis ball that got the better of little Danny Torrance. Kneeling, playing with his miniature cars in a corridor on the second floor of the Overlook, a yellow tennis ball rolls on the orange, brown, and red carpet, patterned like a maze. The ball rolls silently, all the way to the child, interrupting him in his play.

In a shot filmed from behind, we can guess the child's curiosity as he raises his head to look toward the far end of the hotel corridor, framed Kubrickally symmetrical.

No one is there. Who could have thrown the tennis ball? Is he being invited to play? (*Come and play with us.*) Perhaps Danny is thinking about his father as he slowly, hesitantly progresses towards a door left ajar. A red key inserted in the lock. The child calls after his mother, as he enters uncertainly into the forbidden room, room 237. (*Mom? Mom, are you in there?*) After being interrupted in his game, Danny should have most definitely turned and run.

* * *

Wendy Torrance in a hospital bed, listening to Stuart Ullman tell her that her husband's body hasn't been found. As he is about to leave, the Overlook's director gives Danny a yellow tennis ball. In May 1980, on its first week in theatres, the movie's running time was 146 minutes.

Stanley Kubrick wasn't satisfied by the effect created by the original final scene. He cut it from the movie, and reconsidered his conclusion. He gave the order to the projectionists in the nine theatres where the movie was being shown to cut the hospital scene and send the now undesirable piece of film to Warner Studios, the film's distributor. *The Shining* lasts 144 minutes today. Those who saw the movie in the first week saw that now missing scene, and they are lucky viewers.

Jack's Voice

"All right, our first category is French actors…"

Born on December 11, 1930, he was a racecar driver. He became known in 1956 thanks to his work with Brigitte Bardot in Roger Vadim's movie *Et Dieu… créa la femme*. His relationship with the extraordinarily beautiful actress, wife of the director, caused the disintegration of the Vadim/Bardot couple.

Ten years later, he'd play in an Oscar-winning movie by Claude Lelouch, *Un homme et une femme*, which also won the Palme d'Or in Cannes that year. He would marry the actor and director Nadine Marquand (nee Lucienne Marquand), with whom he would have three children, including Pauline, who wouldn't live past nine months. This family tragedy inspired his wife to create *Ça n'arrive qu'aux autres*, in which he was supposed to play a father mourning his child. The pain still too fresh, he chose to let the Italian actor Marcello Mastroianni play the part.

His son-in-law was, for a time, Bertrand Cantat, front man for the French rock band Noir Désir. This of course to his eventual sorrow, when Marie, his daughter, was murdered by her husband.

"Jean-Louis Trintignant?"

He is the voice behind Jack Nicholson's character in the

French version of *The Shining*. Stanley Kubrick chose the actor himself. Kubrick wanted absolute control over the smallest details of his productions.

A Gust of Wind

You divide your time between the college—you're still teaching—and the hospital. Eleven days already since tragic events set your world upside down. Eleven days already, and *only* eleven days, you think, completely disoriented. Every slice of twenty-four hours seems like an eternity, it's charged with emotion and constant delicate decisions to make; you feel like you've been in the eye of the storm for months.

There is the trying shock of seeing the one in whom your own life began forty-two years ago pass by, right in front of you, splayed out on a stretcher. You were pacing the corridor of the emergency room at the hospital when by chance you saw her being transported right past you, on a stretcher, pale and unconscious, coming from an examination room where X-rays rendered the extent of the damage in black and white. Rolled right in front of you towards the intensive care unit.

You didn't even recognize her when she was wheeled by; she was in such bad shape, just ravaged. She looked a hundred, a thousand years old. She used to be so beautiful. You understand from then on that you'll never be able to find peace in her comforting arms again. You weren't allowed into the intensive care unit for several interminable hours. An antidote was injected into her, an attempt to clean her system from the medication she swallowed the day before, a forever damned February 11, after your last conversation. A considerable quantity of pills. The damage might end up being irreversible in the eventuality that, by some sort of miracle, she might be saved.

In the depths of her emotional quagmire, your mother forgot that a physiotherapist was supposed to come on Tuesday morning for a series of rehabilitation exercises for her left hip. To relearn how to walk, with the help of an orthopedic instrument. Knock, knock, knock! No answer. After a few knocks, the physio turned towards the neighbour who was poking her nose out from behind her door.

Hesitant at first, your mother's friend ended up yielding to the physio's insistent demands that she open the door with your mother's spare key. Carmen had a choice to make: either agree to the order, or the physio would call emergency services to break down her neighbour's door. Smash right through it with an axe, you can't help but think.

A credit card cut into pieces, right next to a pair of scissors, foreshadowed the worst. Your mother's body was stretched out on a bed, over the sheets—they weren't even undone. Bottle after bottle after bottle of pills, all empty. The paramedics would grab them as they left to help the emergency room doctors give the proper treatment. They took the pills as evidence. But there's no letter. So, it looks like you'll have to fill in the gaps yourself. But you know the major plot points of this story already. By casting a dark veil over the wretched memories of her childhood, your mother took with her part of her own memory as well. You had a blessed childhood, back before you could remember any of it. When a mother disappears, it is the definite suppression of a large portion of the first years of a life.

Black Hole

Carmen didn't call you Monday evening to tell you about your mother's decision to kill herself. She made a choice, with serious and dire consequences. She made the choice not to warn you. She could have. What a choice. You wonder, without being able to come up with a convincing answer, how this woman could have, just a few hours later, watched her *stories* on television, before placing her dentures in a glass of water, slipping under her sheets, and sleeping like a baby. On the other side of the wall separating their bedrooms, her best friend slipped towards death.

What weighs more heavily? The betrayal of a promise made to someone you care about? Or the definitive loss of a friend? Where does the mediocrity of indifference begin?

Why didn't Carmen call you on Monday night to tell you about your mother's ghastly project? Out of compassion? Out of true friendship? Out of respect for a friend who was sick of living, who wanted to cut short the agony of a future she anticipated?

Had she sounded the alarm by calling you: you could have at least tried to do something for your mother. You could have brought her to a psychiatrist, supported her, stood beside her, bought her a motorized wheelchair to make it easier for her to move about, hired professional help, visited more often, called more often, invited her to the restaurant, written letters to her, flooded her with pictures of her lovely granddaughter, told her about your best memories from childhood—because of course there were some—told her you loved her, looked her in the eyes, not looked away, no, looked her straight in the eyes to the depths of her soul cut deep by the sharp blade of the past and told her again and again that you loved her.

And since that day, you truly hate Carmen who stumbled through the last hours of the one who gave birth to you. You hate the old woman, since out of futile loyalty, she robbed you of a last opportunity to make your mother's life easier to bear. On the contrary: she involuntarily presented you with the impossible decision of executing, a few days later, the power of attorney she had taken time to swear out with a notary ten years earlier.

Ekki Múkk

Eyelids purple, veins terrible and popping, she was im- mured in silence as heavy as a tombstone. I patiently watched over Mom, awaiting her death. For three days I sat next to her bed where she endured undue protrac- tion of her agony, swallowed by the dim light of an anony- mous hospital room. A hospital room where everything would end in a matter of hours. They reassured me about her state nonetheless; critical, but stable. Her kidneys no longer worked, we had to expect she'd pass from one moment to the next. Regular doses of morphine dulled her pain and sent her into a sort of calm sleep. I could feel pain and sadness for this woman and could only see awful reasons that might explain her presence in this antechamber of death.

I fell asleep at some point. A few hours at a time inter- spersed with watching her breathe. A deep inhalation accom- panied by a wheeze, then a quick exhalation. The pulmonary metronome, the single perceptible evidence of life. Hour after hour, infinitesimally, the interval lengthened.

Time seemed to be shaped by the rhythm of shift changes. I was gently pressed a few times to go back home to rest a lit- tle, freshen up, get my mind off things. "You'll end up getting sick if you stay here. And anyway, in the state your mother is in, she won't know the difference. She might even be waiting to be alone to pass, that happens frequently." (I thought we always heard the opposite?) "She doesn't even know you're there." (And usually they tell you that coma patients hear everything around them.) How can you know, in the end?

These slight inconveniences represented nothing at all compared to what awaited my mother around the corner. My humble and uncomfortable silence was my last demonstration of solidarity. I would have gladly slept on the hospital floor if it could have changed anything. It was out of the question, of course I'd be with her in her last moments, she who took me in her arms at my first minute of life.

Towards five in the morning on Sunday, February 24, Mom opened her eyes and seemed to regain consciousness. It could be the nurses disturbed her as they busied themselves around her in her hospital bed. They might have accidently woken Mom up. I took advantage of the moment to lean over her. Her eyes fixed on me and she seemed to recognize me. A spark of intelligence in her eyes, an unforeseen moment of lucidity.

I smiled, stroked her grey hair, told her I loved her, that she could go. Her whole face seemed to express her love, her regrets, her last wishes. And we looked at each other in silence for a few blessed moments. A whole life, to reach this one final communion. Then, hoping to brighten her spirits, to give her the faintest moment of light, I told her that the next day, February 25, her granddaughter Aurore would turn seven, it was her birthday. I secretly hoped that Mom would hold on 'til Tuesday not to lay a dark mark on the date for the rest of both my life and my daughter's. Or that she might pass now, quickly, on Sunday, saving her from meaningless pain.

I couldn't be entirely sure, but I was convinced she understood the essentials of what I was saying: her face lit up like I hoped it would and she opened her mouth. Even if no sound could come out, I chose to believe that her wordless plea was for me to take her in my arms.

Using this momentary lucidity, I grabbed my iPod out of my back pocket. I chose a piece by Sigur Rós. I placed the device against her left ear and let my mother bask in that celestial music one last time. Seven minutes and forty-two seconds of listening, her eyes opened and stared into mine. Beyond the Icelandic lyrics completely incomprehensible to us we felt, I'm sure of it, the rare importance of the moment. Saying goodbye to your mother marks a man's spirit. Despite her advanced dehydration, a single tear ran down her right eye to her pillow. Ekki Múkk. Not a sound.

Unreal
You appeared to me
To no other
And became nothing

Fragile, prey to omnipresent doubts, she had the humility of her own limits, her most evident failures. She was a mix of intuition, desperate solitude, and feminine sensitivity. Human chaos in all its splendor. In that, at least, she wasn't different at all from every other neurotic mother, I supposed.

In the end, she realized that the worst prisons aren't built of stone, but of our own actions, or the ones we are subjected to, and smother us, slowly. Prisoner of herself, of her own past, she was swallowed by a crime committed seventy years ago.

We hold our breath
As long as
We can achieve
We close our eyes
And hold our hands against our ears
We hear no sound

I was dozing on my chair when I realized my mother hadn't breathed in a while. Then a rattle from beyond the grave startled me. Followed by a deep exhalation. The last. After a moment, a minute maybe, I came near her. And for what seemed like an eternity, I gazed at death which, I realized, had come to tear away the last parcel of life my mom still had.

I stayed there, in silence. I thought back to the happy moments beside her. Mom running behind me on my bicycle for the very first time, Mom applauding a fair ball right down the line into right field, Mom waving to me as I spun before her on a merry-go-round, Mom taking pictures of me among dozens of other children as I blow out the five candles of a birthday cake, eyes filled with tenderness, Mom holding my Aurore at the birthing home, Mom handing me a chocolate ice cream cone, Mom helping me paint the cupboards of my first apartment in the big city, Mom pushing me on the swing, at the park, Mom disinfecting my knee with mercurochrome, seated next to me on the side of the bathtub, my small wounded leg next to hers.

Walking backwards, I left the room as silently as possible, respectfully. Footstep after footstep, looking at her the whole time, I closed the door and walked, emptied of all substance, towards the nursing station.

Breathing
Heartbeats
Breathe and dive down
Ekki múkk. Not a sound.
(Sigur Rós)

Mom passed seemingly peacefully in the night between Monday and Tuesday. On February 26, at one in the morning.

Broken Family

As Wendy Torrance climbs the stairs backwards, holding her baseball bat for protection, her husband Jack reveals, as if speaking to an accomplice, his projects imbued with morbid undertones, auguring nothing good for little Danny: "I think we should discuss what should be done with him."

It's likely in these terms that Hansel and Gretel's spineless father was convinced to abandon his children in the forest by the evil stepmother. We all know that the old fairytale goes far beyond the story of a labyrinthine path recognized thanks to a few breadcrumbs. It is, in fact, a horrible story of child abuse that ends up in a failed attempt at cannibalism.

These days, not a week goes by without the media giving us some sensational story of family tragedy: a man barricades himself in his house, threatening to put an end to his life; a father sees his life fall apart before him when he discovers his children drowned in the bathtub and, in the cold conjugal bed, the body of his wife who swallowed every last pill of her bottle of Celexa antidepressants; or the jealous ex-husband who guns down his wife and the man she left him for only a month earlier with his Browning 5.25; or another man who, after an argument, shatters his wife's skull with his Stanley hammer.

And how many cars collide with the roadside railing without ever braking? They slip under the radar, no one calls them infanticides plus the suicide of a desperate parent at the wheel.

"*You wouldn't ever hurt Mummy and me, would you?*" Danny Torrance asks his father.

Bloody Jacques

I'd want him to hear me speak. I'd want my words to have the same effect on him as gasoline poured on a gagged and bound hostage, prisoner in an old shed.

We'll never know at what age he began to suspect that a monster was hiding in a shrouded corner of his mind. At first, did Jacques Forest consider this destructive presence like a marginal, abstract entity? Did the monster first begin to stretch and move and heave when his conscience was crushed by the liberating weight of sleep? Orphaned young, taken in by a neighbour, Stanislas Dupuis, did little Jacques feel a chasm between himself and other kids his age?

It's altogether impossible, obviously, to excuse the murder of his wife in front of his two five-year-old daughters. But I can't help thinking about what might have pushed him over the edge, into the deep darkness of the human mind. Understanding my grandfather might be beyond my abilities, but at least I'd like to find a way to rationally apprehend the issue of his criminal mind. I believe we all carry within us, to varying degrees, a portion of shadow, a portion of dark. Like an essential flaw, with my grandfather being the timing belt in the Forest family: a murder, a disappearance, two suicides. What else?

Some claim this flaw is not a trait shared by all of us. Not me. We've all had at least one shameful night of weakness, even in some cases a breakdown. But we quickly, very quickly, close the door that was ajar, terrified at what we saw. We prefer to remain on the threshold and, hypocritically, comfort ourselves with the thought that true deviance is only for madmen and lunatics, instead of worrying about this troubling truth: Evil unites us as much as Good does. Maybe more. After all, Evil, even in its most extreme manifestation as horror, is, in the end, by its frequency and universality, something rather banal.

But I want to go back to my grandfather, Jacques Forest, my obsessive enigma. Did alcohol debase him? Nervous depression? Guided by an unstable demon, obeying this voice that lived in him, his murderous arm sought to spill blood, spill blood until it flowed in rivers and torrents in the gutters and furrows of his small, god-forsaken village.

By his hand, two five-year-old girls would not be able to harbour illusions for very long. The red spatter spurting out of the shattered skull of their mother stained *forever, and ever, and ever* the blue of their innocent eyes. Like maggots filling a forgotten corpse, black thoughts invaded my mother's mind from the day she glimpsed the implements of hell in the ghastly shape of a bloody hammer.

Had he lived in our time, Jacques Forest might have disappeared in the jungle of junkies, alcoholics potholed by Cutty Sark, ex-prisoners and pimps you find in every big city. He would have probably realized the evil potential that simmered in the mind of this pathetic scumbag with the well-heeled appearance of a peaceful country doctor. Or perhaps, on the contrary, he would have been bafflingly boring, like the interchangeable and improvised actors of our regular conjugal dramas that make the front page of our tabloids.

Now that my mother is dead, it is my turn to have my

mind shrouded by the splendor of the total eclipse of this new Dr. Jekyll. I try as best I can to give meaning to my life. Due to the heinous actions of my forbearer Jacques Forest, our family speaks the same language as nations and history. The language of Kubrick-red violence.

Others can invest fortunes in therapy if they wish. I clumsily try to convince myself that it's possible to win the fight, to slay the Minotaur hidden in the heart of the labyrinth, and spit in death's eye. Fuck you, Dr. Jacques! But he doesn't hear me. He's too busy hanging from a rope looped around a beam in the shed behind his damned house on 21 Main Street where, ironically, a killer actually lived.

A Permanent Mark

One of the most difficult things to do after a loved one passes is to clean and empty their home. As executor of Mom's will, the task fell to me. I set myself the goal of going through her things in a day. Despite my mother's almost ascetic lifestyle, despite the fact she lived in a modest three-room apartment, it took me almost three days.

I began with her papers, leaving the bigger stuff for later. I kept what I thought might be useful for her death certificate, and threw most everything else in the recycling bin—obsolete or useless documents: the guarantee for an old Electrolux vacuum cleaner that she no longer even owned, a few home insurance contracts, long since expired, notices of assessment from the revenue agency and other declarations of revenue going as far back as 1980, notarized divorce papers dating back to 1976, and much, much more. Seeing her entire life in these legal documents did provide an advantage: that of making the task seem foreign, bureaucratic. Removing its potential for melodrama.

The second day, I went through her personal belongings. I threw pretty much everything that couldn't be recycled or given to charity in the building's large bin. I remember wondering whether my mother's life could be summed up by bureaucratic wrangling and a pile of worthless artifacts. I went back and forth perhaps twenty times between her apartment and the basement with the garbage and recycling bins. A material life summarized by twenty-two garbage bags and two car-fulls of stuff. That's what we are.

In the living room, I gathered everything that could still be useful, taking care to split the objects into two piles, separated by a rocking chair in the middle of the room: on one end, what could be kept or given to members of the family (the television set, appliances, a lot of DVDs, CDs, and even more cassettes, laminated or framed children's pictures, various useful objects, her favourite recipe book). On the other, articles destined for the Society of Saint Vincent de Paul (clothes, furniture, dishes, kitchen equipment, non-perishable goods). A tough moment to go through. I kept having to hold and sort objects that used to have sentimental value to my mom. I was smashed by wave after wave of emotion. A year earlier, I would have said you were crazy if you told me I would well up when I smelled a quilt. And yet... The effect of an old elementary school project or a faded card drawn by the hand of a child can be quite extraordinary.

I went through everything meticulously, telling myself I was spending a few last privileged moments with her. I began to believe that the objects we possess carry with them a mark of some sort, our past. Without seeking out the mysteries of my mother's life, I reminded myself to be attentive to the small details that might have some importance in her eyes, a sort of mute homage to her memory. I kept the boxes of photographs for the end, in order to close this painful episode with as much masochistic pathos as possible. Losing myself in the old pictures, I rediscovered happy days spent with her, cursing myself for never having appreciated their value when it mattered. And I asked myself what our lives would have looked like if I hadn't had an ungrateful heart.

Lloyd and Me

Interior – Hotel Ballroom and Corridor – Medium Shot

I walk along the corridor in a fancy hotel, turn left and walk across the ballroom to the bar. Soft red light. CAMERA tracks me, revealing a room filled to the brim with people in their most elegant dress. I sit at the bar. The barman holds himself straight in front of me, as if he was expecting me. He smiles discreetly, and will do so throughout the scene. Maybe he's been smiling exactly like this for his whole life.

  (rest of the scene in close-up shot)

  Lloyd
Good evening, Mister Forest.

  Cut to:

  Me
Good evening, Lloyd. But let me just correct you: it isn't Forest, it's Roy.

  Cut to:

  Lloyd
If you say so, sir. As you wish. If you'll allow me, it's been quite some time since we've had the pleasure of seeing you.

Cut to:

ME
Unfortunately, I've been busy with family responsibilities, these days. You know, the contingencies of life and death. As the expression goes *to be back from the dead...* But anyway, I'm back, dear friend. And you know you're still the best goddamn barman, Lloyd. From Timbuctoo to Portland, Maine—Portland, Oregon for that matter.

· *Lloyd places a bowl of olives and peanuts on the counter in front of me.*

Cut to:

LLOYD
I'm glad you're here, sir.

Cut to:

ME
Glad to be back, Lloyd.

Cut to:

LLOYD
What'll it be, sir?

Cut to:

Something to fight fire with fire, Lloyd.

Cut to:

LLOYD
Can I offer you a drink then, sir?

Cut to:

ME
That's a great idea! Bravo!

I grab a handful of peanuts and toss them in a single fluid movement into my mouth. Lloyd drops a few ice cubes in a glass.

Cut to:

Lloyd preparing a drink. Jack Daniel's. He'll never blink. His sibylline smile will never leave his thin lips.

Cut to:

Lloyd pours rum in the glass. I take my wallet out of my jacket pocket. Lloyd raises his hand straight and firm.

LLOYD
It's on the house, Mister Roy.

Cut to:

I look at Lloyd with a dubious air.

ME
Free? And to what, dare I ask, do I owe such treatment?

Cut to:

LLOYD
Your money is worth nothing here, sir.

Cut to:

I glance at my wallet, then back at Lloyd.

Cut to:

LLOYD
House rules, sir.

Cut to:

I place the wallet back in my back pocket, suspiciously glancing up at Lloyd.

ME
House rules, you say?

Cut to:

LLOYD
Drink, Mister Roy.

Cut to:

ME
I'm the sort of person who likes to know who's paying for his drinks, Lloyd.

Cut to:

LLOYD
That question is none of your concern, Mister Roy—at least not just yet.

Cut to:

I give Lloyd a smile and raise my glass of rum.

ME
As you wish, Lloyd.

Cut to:

LLOYD
Did you ever think, sir, that if you'd gone to her apartment one hour earlier, on that Tuesday in February, you'd be the one who found her in her bed?

Cut to:

ME
That's all I think about these days, Lloyd. I imagine myself knocking, knocking, knocking on her door, not knowing whether she's home or not. *Danielle, I'm home!* I would have asked the concierge to open the door, and then...

Cut to:

LLOYD
I see. But don't you think about it anymore? Do you

remember, sir, what the psychologist whom you saw for ten years used to say? She said you should be careful, that it was an explosive situation. You remember the weekly visits to the shrink, don't you, Mister Roy?

Cut to:

I watch Lloyd, partly intrigued, partly fascinated.

ME
No, I'm sorry, I don't. I don't even have a vague memory of them...but let's get down to brass tacks, if you will. What would be, according to you, this explosive situation, Lloyd?

Cut to:

LLOYD
Not according to me, Mister Roy. According to your psychologist. She warned you that there was some manipulation in what your mother did with her constant threats to end her life. She asked you who, in truth, you were trying to save. Because your mother, sir, reminded your psychologist of the people who, in the midst of drowning, are given a hand to grab onto. And instead of pulling themselves up, they pull you down with them into the abyss. But perhaps that's what you wanted in the end, Mister Roy. After all, the apple doesn't fall far from the tree, if you see what I mean.... As the damned poet said, *your gene pool in your satchel.*

Cut to:

ME

I've got to say you intrigue me, Lloyd. I don't have the faintest memory of these sessions. I swear. Would you be teasing me, Lloyd? Are you the sort of man to poke fun at your customers?

Cut to:

LLOYD

I wouldn't dare, sir. I've never been in the habit. You can be sure of it. But may I ask you an... indiscreet question, sir?

Cut to:

ME

It depends. But go ahead, and I'll tell you whether I want to answer it or not. I'm listening, Lloyd.

Cut to:

LLOYD

At the time, did you blame your mother? Are you still mad at her, perhaps? But maybe that's a bit too indiscreet, sir. Please, don't answer if you feel I've pushed the limit of good taste with my question, sir.

Cut to:

ME

Not at all, Lloyd. You question is entirely legitimate. Honestly, it's still hard to say. I was wounded, run through with a sharp blade, you can understand. But if I was her, I might have done the same thing. At least, I would have been tempted. The only thing that stops me from claiming with absolute certainty that I would have done it is that I don't know if I would have had the *courage* to do it.

Cut to:

LLOYD
Not to be disagreeable, sir, but we both know you absolutely have what it takes to go through with it...

Cut to:

ME
But to come back to your question, Lloyd, whether I'm still mad at her. It's funny, but I don't see it from that angle. Asking the question like you do, well, it makes it quite self-centred. Always bringing her death back to me, me, me.

Cut to:

LLOYD
That would be normal, though, wouldn't it? And it wouldn't be...unexpected for you to react in such a way, if I may speak freely and with all due respect, sir.

Cut to:

ME
But I can't blame her in relation to me. It's more the fact that she planted a seed in our family, she planted the idea

that suicide is an option, one worth considering when everything seems dark. That's what screws with me like you can't imagine, Lloyd. For example, if one day my daughter tries to take her own life, I would blame my mother, I'd dig her up and piss on her urn while chanting demonic incantations. I would hold her, even beyond the grave, criminally responsible. If ever...if ever...I'd damn her to the day I die, Lloyd. And I would rush down to Hell, Lloyd, willingly, to kill my mother again and again, if one day...

I swallow a mouthful of Jack Daniel's and brush aside a lock of my hair that has fallen into my eyes, red with rage.

Dissolve to:

KDK12 to KDK1

As I was going through Mom's stuff, I made sure to keep a full evening to go through the numerous pictures she kept in disarray in old shoeboxes. Since I would never again spend time at her place, pinot noir felt rather appropriate. More recent photographs, those taken over the past dozen years, were naturally familiar to me. Most of them were pictures I had sent her from time to time by mail or given to her in person. Pictures almost invariably containing my little Aurore's irresistible smile. Here she was as a newborn, here a toddler in diapers, her belly nice and round and smooth. Playing in a park, giving a hug to some fuzzy mascot, or unwrapping a Christmas present. Every celebration was included, another reason for pictures: hunting for Easter eggs, birthdays with multicoloured balloons, flutes and tiny birthday hats, witches and princesses and fairies for Halloween. Followed by family reunions, outings at the sugar shack, decorating the Christmas tree, New Year's Eve.

Examining the pictures, if I put aside recent events, I could almost convince myself that Mom had managed to slay her demons. But it was clear now, that even in the last few years, in her moments of solitude she was dealing with the fatal weight of the mute tragedy playing over and over again in her head. Mom must have lived in such a pathological state that her tormented mind had turned against itself, become a force of self-destruction. The contrast between her smiling in the picture with Aurore, and her swallowing countless pills on that Monday night in February told me all I needed to know about the silent weight she carried with her. A little bit like a cancer whose metastasis has taken over an organ. My mother let herself be eaten away by an obsessive thought, her mind shattering in waves on the seawall of her personal tragedy.

Revisiting those events of September 1942 sent her into a descending spiral that seemed to her impossible to stop. A maze without an exit. Dead end. As if the mental distress grew to the point of having nowhere to go, taking over her whole life, feeding itself with itself and its irrational exuberance. When the air becomes stale, you end up breathless. It's easy to imagine that Mom lived the last moments of her life *in camera*, in a hotel buried by snow that muffled every sound. It fell, ceaselessly. And communications with the Overlook were definitely cut off. The more the snow fell, as the storm continued, the more Mom was imprisoned in the vise of her mind.

"KDK12 to KDK1. I repeat: KDK12 to KDK1 . . ."
Nothing but static.

* * *

I worked through most of the bottle of pinot, but, seated in the loveseat, I went on with my attentive examination of each picture which constituted, in a way, Mom's personal museum. One of them grabbed my attention more than the others. A black-and-white picture. Square. White border. A smiling couple seated in a field of wheat. No idea who might have taken the picture. Jacques Forest holding his darling by the waist, while blond Aurore leans on her husband, right arm over the left shoulder of the man who, in all honesty, does bear a striking resemblance to the French actor Bernard Giraudeau. The young doctor is nibbling on a wheat stalk. He's dressed simply, in dark pants and a light shirt, its sleeves rolled up. She's wearing a summer dress, seated knees bent on her husband's jacket, with a carefully placed hat on her head, draping her eyes in shadow. The two of them are looking straight at the photographer, with all the frivolity of youth. The woman's slightly swollen belly betrays her few months of pregnancy.

On the back of this pretty black-and-white picture, a short handwritten message, signed by *Your Jack*: "The rays of your eyes as blue as the sky, Aurore, shine on me like heavenly verse. Thank you for choosing me." If we are to believe what's written on the back, the picture must have been taken on a carefree day in August 1936. A Sunday, if we are to judge by their attire, but I've got no proof of that.

Happy Mother's Day

Int. Apartment & Bathroom

The CAMERA TRACKS LEFT-RIGHT across the room to an open door. The CAMERA SLOWLY progresses through the bathroom's door frame. The CAMERA STOPS ITS MOVEMENT. The DOOR is now completely open. At the far end of the room, an OLD WOMAN is seated in a bathtub behind a shower curtain. The bathtub's water is marred by red. She pulls the curtain with her right hand and stares at me unblinkingly. Nothing threatening, but nothing welcoming in that long stare.

Cut to:

Medium shot. The woman climbs out of the bathtub and steps slowly in my direction.

Cut to:

Close-up shot. I walk towards the woman.

Cut to:

Medium shot. The woman takes me in her wet arms. I see in the mirror in front of us that she is holding a razor blade stained with blood in her right hand. Her suppurating skin has taken on a greenish tint, the sign of putrefaction.

Cut to:

Close-up shot. I bend towards her to whisper a secret in her ear.

A Door Pushed Open

That Nietzsche quote: "When you gaze long into the abyss, the abyss gazes also into you." Sometimes a simple phrase plants a seed in your brain, and never leaves.

A friend of mine lost her brother five years ago (hanging), then her father a year later (hunting rifle). She wrote to tell me that a psychologist warned her to take care of herself and hold her own darkness at bay. When a suicide occurs in the family, she warned me in turn, it's often a door pushed open. We must be careful not to follow, and cross the Rubicon. It seems in fact that, without being hereditary, the suicide of a loved one makes us into potential candidates. At risk.

When a hurricane makes landfall, it leaves behind considerable destruction. Some vehicles are considered total losses after an accident. Life isn't a sugar-coated fairytale. Never let your guard down. Always remain vigilant. Stay on code red. Kubrick red, of course. Over my head, the sun strives to foil the clouds.

Solitude is Dangerous

Solitude is dangerous. Over a prolonged period, it forces man to face himself, to meditate on his own fate, on his destiny. If an individual has nihilistic tendencies, solitude can drag him into the abyss of desperate thoughts.

Solitude is dangerous. Over a prolonged period, it forces man to face himself, to meditate on his own fate, on his destiny. If an individual has nihilistic tendencies, solitude can drag him into the abyss of desperate thoughts.

Solitude is dangerous. Over a prolonged period, it forces man to face himself, to meditate on his own fate, on his destiny. If an individual has nihilistic tendencies, solitude can drag him into the abyss of desperate thoughts.

Solitude is dangerous. Over a prolonged period, it forces man to face himself, to meditate on his own fate, on his destiny. If an individual has nihilistic tendencies, solitude can drag him into the abyss of desperate thoughts.

Solitude is dangerous. Over a prolonged period, it forces man to face himself, to meditate on his own fate, on his destiny. If an individual has nihilistic tendencies, solitude can drag him into the abyss of desperate thoughts.

Solitude is dangerous. Over a prolonged period, it forces man to face himself, to meditate on his own fate, on his destiny. If an individual has nihilistic tendencies, solitude can drag him into the abyss of desperate thoughts.

Solitude is dangerous. Over a prolonged period, it forces man to face himself, to meditate on his own fa42te, on his destiny. If an individual has nihilistic tendencies, solitude can drag him into the abyss of desperate thoughts.

Solitude is dangerous. Over a prolonged period, it forces man to face himself, to meditate on his own fate, on his destiny. If an individual has nihilistic tendencies, solitude can drag him into the abyss of desperate thoughts.

Solitude is dangerous. Over a prolonged period, it forces man to face himself, to meditate on his own fate, on his destiny. If an individual has nihilistic tendencies, solitude can drag him into the abyss of desperate thoughts.

Solitude is dangerous. Over a prolonged period, it forces man to face himself, to meditate on his own fate, on his destiny. If an individual has nihilistic tendencies, solitude can drag him into the abyss of desperate thoughts.

Solitude is dangerous. Over a prolonged period, it forces man to face himself, to meditate on his own fate, on his destiny. If an individual has nihilistic tendencies, solitude can drag him into the abyss of desperate thoughts.

Solitude is dangerous. Over a prolonged period, it forces man to face himself, to meditate on his own fate, on his destiny. If an individual has nihilistic tendencies, solitude can drag him into the abyss of desperate thoughts.

Abraham's Arm

Jack's encounter in the washroom next to the ball-room determines what occurs next. The mission endowed by the ghostly employee of the Overlook Hotel, Delbert Grady, marks a point of no return in Jack's ghoulish project of eliminating his son. Perceived as a punishment as much as a challenge to his paternal authority, this mandate gives Jack an almost biblical mission. It's now clear he no longer has a choice: he will have to execute his only son on the Overlook's altar.

Kubrick seems to be suggesting a wrathful God out of the Old Testament in the scene where we see Jack Torrance overlooking the model of the maze in which Wendy and Danny are strolling. Do we see mother and son from Jack's point of view, or are we viewing a far-overhead shot, a celestial one? Roger Ebert, the movie critic, talked about this in his review of the movie: which of *The Shining*'s characters can be considered a reliable observer? Whose version of events can the viewer trust?

Repressed Scene

A mother, her son

Exterior hotel – Maze – Day, medium shot

From the hotel they just exited, the mother runs after the son, towards the maze. THE CAMERA PANS LEFT-RIGHT AND TRACKS with them to entrance to Maze.

MOTHER
The loser has to keep America clean, how's that?

SON
All right.

MOTHER
And you're going to lose. And I'm going to get you—you better run fast! Look out—I'm coming in close.

The child and mother run into the maze.

THE CHILD (OFF)
You'll have to keep America clean.

(Like an excerpt from the script of an imaginary movie, scene 42)

Thanks and Яegяets

This book owes its existence to a few people, most of whom happily (at least as far as I know) don't stalk the corridors of hotels, axe in hand.

I'll start by thanking my Grandmother Jeanine Roy, who was the first to tell me about Dr. Forest's ghastly story. Impossible! Surely grandma was off her rocker! She wasn't as young as she used to be, Jeanine! And yet...

Through his sometimes harsh and uncompromising words, but always encouraging, Robert Lévesque forced me not to turn away, to look at tragedy where it actually lay: the terrifying corridor of the Overlook's West Wing. And in my own memories.

A very theatrical thanks to all the Lloyds who helped me see, on a few nights sprinkled with red rum, the other side of the mirror. Look at where it's led us...

More seriously, I regret the fact that Stanley Kubrick will never be able to read this text. *Kubrick Red* is a tortured homage to the brilliant, perfectionist filmmaker. I can only get as close to him as those who were closest to him. I'd like this text to one day end up in the hands of Michel Ciment, *the* great Kubrick specialist. More than that, I hope this book will one day end up in Ms. Kubrick's hands. This book is for you, too, Christiane Harlan.

And, finally, I want to most particularly thank the master, the master architect of torturous mazes, *the great* Stanley Kubrick.

—S.R.